THE WRITER'S OPTIONS

THE WRITER'S OPTIONS

Lessons in Style and Arrangement
Seventh Edition

Max Morenberg
Miami University

Jeff Sommers
Miami University—Middletown

with

Donald A. Daiker
Miami University

Andrew Kerek
The American University in Cairo

New York   San Francisco   Boston
London   Toronto   Sydney   Tokyo   Singapore   Madrid
Mexico City   Munich   Paris   Cape Town   Hong Kong   Montreal

Vice President/Editor in Chief: Joe Terry
Senior Acquisitions Editor: Steven Rigolosi
Development Editor: Barbara Santoro
Senior Marketing Manager: Melanie Craig
Senior Supplements Editor: Donna Campion
Production Manager: Charles Annis
Project Coordination, Text Design, and Electronic Page Makeup: Pre-Press Company, Inc.
Cover Designer/Manager: Nancy Danahy
Cover Photo: PhotoDisc/Getty Images, Inc.
Manufacturing Buyer: Roy Pickering
Printer and Binder: Courier Corporation
Cover Printer: Phoenix Color Corp.

Library of Congress Cataloging-in-Publication Data

The writer's options: lessons in style and arrangement.-- 7th ed. / Max Morenberg, Jeff
Sommers; with Donald A. Daiker, Andrew Kerek.
     p. cm.
   Includes index.
   ISBN 0-321-07226-X (alk. paper)
     1. English language--Rhetoric. 2. Report writing. I. Morenberg, Max, 1940-
II. Sommers, Jeffrey.

PE1408 .W7716 2002
808'.042--dc21

2002040571

Please visit our website at http://www.ablongman.com

ISBN 0-321-07226-X

   4 5 6 7 8 9 BKM BKM   0 9 8 7 6 5 4

BRIEF CONTENTS

DETAILED CONTENTS

PREFACE

The purpose of *The Writer's Options: Lessons in Style and Arrangement*, Seventh Edition, is to help your students become better writers. The book assumes that writers become better by practicing writing and rewriting and by learning to recognize the language options available so that they can choose the best sentence, paragraph, and essay strategies to make their point. The exercises allow your students to practice revising by arranging sentences, paragraphs, and essays in many different ways. Doing the exercises will help students master new constructions and make writing decisions in terms of context and purpose. Because there are usually multiple "right" answers, the exercises encourage students to play with words and phrases, to experiment with language, and to explore new ways to express feelings and ideas. Students will learn how to craft prose and how to slow down and look at text the way writers look at text.

✨ ORGANIZATION

The Writer's Options: Lessons in Style and Arrangement is organized into three main parts:

- Part One: Lessons in the Writing Process: Composing and Combining
- Part Two: Lessons in Style: Revising Sentences
- Part Three: Lessons in Rearrangement: Revising Whole Drafts

Part One, which includes two lessons, offers an overview of the writing process and an introduction to sentence combining. Each lesson in **Part Two** and **Part Three** begins with a Preview, new to this edition, which offers a quick sketch of the main ideas in that unit. After the Preview, an introductory section explains a revision strategy that focuses on sentences, paragraphs, or entire drafts, and illustrates its use. The introductory sections are important to read and think about. But it is the exercises that are the essence of each lesson—and of the book: The exercises provide actual practice in composing and revising. The draft-length exercises—those with titles like "A Fair to Remember," "Of Gems, Kings, and Curses," and "Rhyme and Reason"—are especially important because they require combining sets of short sentences into paragraphs or drafts, and thus provide a specific context for writing practice.

The draft-length exercises alternate with other types of exercises that help your students practice basic constructing patterns, creative patterns, and various revising strategies. By working out the basic constructing exercise before doing the first full-length exercise in any lesson, students can test their mastery of that unit's strategy. The creating exercises take students one step farther: They ask writers to expand sentences by using the strategy taught in that lesson to add details of their own. The creating exercises encourage students to transfer their new skills into actual writing. Additional types of exercises both add variety to the book and provide practice in different writing tasks.

The book's lessons stand alone: They neither refer to other lessons nor explicitly build on one another. This is a deliberate choice on our part, a choice that offers you more flexibility in using *The Writer's Options: Lessons in Style and Arrangement.* While the book will help your students if they work through it from the beginning, feel free to move from lesson to lesson in ways that will best serve the objectives of your writing course. The book can provide the structure for an entire semester's course, but it can also readily fit into the already-determined structure of an existing course.

℘ FEATURES NEW TO THE SEVENTH EDITION

The Writer's Options has developed slowly, in three- and four-year cycles, since the first edition appeared in 1978. We have tried to improve the text with every new edition. The seventh edition is no exception: It offers new features that are designed to help students move through each chapter more efficiently and write more effectively.

- **Chapter Previews:** Each lesson begins with a brief Preview of the unit to give students guideposts to what they will learn in the lesson.
- **Updated Exercises and Examples:** We replaced over 100 examples, short exercises, and full-length exercises we thought were out-of-date or overly familiar. New exercises represent gender, ethnic, and cultural diversity to reflect the diverse experiences of all students taking this course.

- **More Focused Part and Chapter Titles:** New titles for each of *The Writer's Options'* three parts now clearly emphasize the book's major focuses: the writing process, style, and arrangement. Plus, in this edition all chapters are labeled as "Lessons" instead of units, reminding students of the book's subtitle: "Lessons in Style and Arrangement."
- **New Exercise:** "Lesson 1: Inventing and Drafting" now concludes with a new exercise designed to prompt students to create their own texts, building on information provided in some of the book's exercises.

❧ ENDURING FEATURES

- **Organization:** The text is organized to reflect the usual sequence of the composing process: inventing, drafting, revising. Lesson 1 offers an overview of inventing and drafting along with ideas for getting started. Lesson 2 follows and explains in detail how to use the book effectively. The remaining lessons offer students a variety of revision strategies at the sentence, paragraph, and essay levels.
- **Sentence Combining:** The numerous, varied exercises that conclude each lesson provide students with opportunities to learn revision through sentence combining. Exercises emphasize creating different syntactical structures and revising paragraphs and essays through sentence-combining.

We think you will find the Seventh Edition both familiar in ways that retain the traditional strengths of *The Writer's Options* and new in exciting ways that will make using the book a fresh experience.

❧ BOOK-SPECIFIC SUPPLEMENT

Instructor's Manual   The Instructor's Manual provides additional resources, suggestions, and exercises designed for both the novice and experienced instructor. Please contact your Longman representative to request a copy. ISBN: 0-321-07228-6.

❧ THE LONGMAN SUPPLEMENTS PACKAGE

In addition to the instructor's manual, many other skills-based supplements, guides, planners, worksheets, and more are available for both instructors and students. All of these are available either free or at greatly reduced prices.

For Additional Reading and Reference

The Dictionary Deal. Two dictionaries can be shrinkwrapped with this text at a nominal fee. *The New American Webster Handy College Dictionary* is a paperback reference text with more than 100,000 entries. *Merriam-Webster's Collegiate Dictionary*, Tenth Edition, is a hardback reference based on a citation file of more than 14.5 million examples of English words drawn from actual use. For more information on how to shrinkwrap a dictionary with your text, please contact your Longman sales representative.

Penguin Quality Paperback Titles. A series of Penguin paperbacks is available at a significant discount when shrinkwrapped with this text. Some titles available are Toni Morrison's *Beloved*, Julia Alvarez's *How the Garcia Girls Lost Their Accents*, Mark Twain's *Huckleberry Finn, Narrative of the Life of Frederick Douglass*, Harriet Beecher Stowe's *Uncle Tom's Cabin*, Dr. Martin Luther King, Jr.'s *Why We Can't Wait*, and plays by Shakespeare, Miller, and Albee. For a complete list of titles or more information, please contact your Longman sales consultant.

***Twenty-Five Great Essays, Fifty Great Essays,* and *One Hundred Great Essays,* edited by Robert DiYanni.** These alphabetically organized essay collections are published as part of the "Penguin Academics" series of low-cost, high-quality offerings intended for use in introductory college courses. All essays were selected for their teachability, both as models for writing and for their usefulness as springboards for student writing. For more information on how to shrinkwrap one of these anthologies with your text, please contact your Longman sales consultant.

100 Things to Write About. This 100-page book contains 100 individual assignments for writing on a variety of topics and in a wide range of formats, from expressive to analytical. Ask your Longman sales representative for a sample copy. 0-673-98239-4.

Electronic and Online Offerings

The Longman Writer's Warehouse. The innovative and exciting online supplement is the perfect accompaniment to any developmental writing course. Created by developmental English instructors specially for developing writers, The Writer's Warehouse covers every part of the writing process. Also included are journaling capabilities, multimedia activities, diagnostic tests, an interactive handbook, and a complete instructor's manual. The Writer's Warehouse requires no space on your school's server; rather, students complete and store their work on the Longman server, and are able to access it, revise it, and continue working at any time. For more details about how to shrinkwrap a free subscription to The Writer's Warehouse with this text, please consult your Longman sales representative. For a free guided tour of the site, visit **http://longmanwriterswarehouse.com.**

The Writer's ToolKit Plus. This CD-ROM offers a wealth of tutorial, exercise, and reference material for writers. It is compatible with either a PC or Macintosh platform, and is flexible enough to be used either occasionally for practice or regularly in class lab sessions. For information on how to bundle this CD-ROM *free* with your text, please contact your Longman sales representative.

GrammarCoach Software. This interactive tutorial helps students practice the basics of grammar and punctuation through 600 self-grading exercises in such problem areas as fragments, run-ons, and agreement. IBM only: 0-205-26509-X.

For Instructors

Electronic Test Bank for Writing. This electronic test bank features more than 5,000 questions in all areas of writing, from grammar to paragraphing, through essay writing, research, and documentation. With this easy-to-use CD-ROM, instructors simply choose questions from the electronic test bank, then print out the completed test for distribution. CD-ROM: 0-321-08117-X. Print version: 0-321-08486-1.

Competency Profile Test Bank, Second Edition. This series of 60 objective tests covers ten general areas of English competency, including fragments; comma splices and run-ons; pronouns; commas; and capitalization. Each test is available in remedial, standard, and advanced versions. Available as reproducible sheets or in computerized versions. Free to instructors. Paper version: 0-321-02224-6. Computerized IBM: 0-321-02633-0. Computerized Mac: 0-321-02632-2.

Diagnostic and Editing Tests and Exercises, Fifth Edition. This collection of diagnostic tests helps instructors assess students' competence in Standard Written English for the purpose of placement or to gauge progress. Available as reproducible sheets or in computerized versions, and free to instructors. Paper: 0-321-11730-1. CD-ROM: 0-321-11731-X.

ESL Worksheets, Third Edition. These reproducible worksheets provide ESL students with extra practice in areas they find the most troublesome. A diagnostic test and post-test are provided, along with answer keys and suggested topics for writing. Free to adopters. 0-321-07765-2.

Longman Editing Exercises. Fifty-four pages of paragraph editing exercises give students extra practice using grammar skills in the context of longer passages. Free when packaged with any Longman title. 0-205-31792-8. Answer key: 0-205-31797-9.

80 Practices. A collection of reproducible, ten-item exercises that provide additional practices for specific grammatical usage problems, such as comma splices, capitalization, and pronouns. Includes an answer key; free to adopters. 0-673-53422-7.

CLAST Test Package, Fourth Edition. These two 40-item objective tests evaluate students' readiness for the CLAST exams. Strategies for teaching CLAST preparedness are included. Free with any Longman English title. Reproducible sheets: 0-321-01950-4. Computerized IBM version: 0-321-01982-2. Computerized Mac version: 0-321-01983-0.

TASP Test Package, Third Edition. These 12 practice pre-tests and post-tests assess the same reading and writing skills covered in the TASP examination. Free with any Longman English title. Reproducible sheets: 0-321-01959-8. Computerized IBM version: 0-321-01985-7. Computerized Mac version: 0-321-01984-9.

Teaching Online: Internet Research, Conversation, and Composition, Second Edition. Ideal for instructors who have never surfed the Net, this easy-to-follow guide offers basic definitions, numerous examples, and step-by-step information about finding and using Internet sources. Free to adopters. 0-321-01957-1.

Using Portfolios. This supplement offers teachers a brief introduction to teaching with portfolios in composition courses. This essential guide addresses the pedagogical and evaluative use of portfolios, and offers practical suggestions for implementing a portfolio evaluation system in a writing class. 0-321-08412-8.

The Longman Instructor's Planner. This all-in-one resource for instructors includes monthly and weekly planning sheets, to-do lists, student contact forms, attendance rosters, a gradebook, an address/phone book, and a mini-almanac. Ask your Longman sales representative for a free copy. 0-321-09247-3.

For Students

Researching Online, Fifth Edition. A perfect companion for a new age, this indispensable new supplement helps students navigate the Internet. Adapted from *Teaching Online*, the instructor's Internet guide, *Researching Online* speaks directly to students, giving them detailed, step-by-step instructions for performing electronic searches. Available free when shrinkwrapped with this text. 0-321-09277-5.

Learning Together: An Introduction to Collaborative Theory. This brief guide to the fundamentals of collaborative learning teaches students how to work effectively in groups, how to revise with peer response, and how to co-author a paper or report. Shrinkwrapped free with this text. 0-673-46848-8.

A Guide for Peer Response, Second Edition. This guide offers students forms for peer critiques, including general guidelines and specific forms for different stages in the writing process. Also appropriate for freshman-level course. Free to adopters. 0-321-01948-2.

Ten Practices of Highly Successful Students. This popular supplement offers concise tips for a successful career in college, helping students learn crucial study skills. Topics include time management, test-taking, reading critically, stress, and motivation. 0-205-30769-8.

Thinking Through the Test, by D.J. Henry [for Florida adoptions]. This special workbook, prepared specially for students in Florida, offers ample skill and practice exercises to help students prep for the Florida State Exit Exam. Available in two versions: with answers and without answers. Also available: Two laminated grids (one for reading, one for writing) that can serve as handy references for students preparing for the Florida State Exit Exam. To shrinkwrap this workbook free with your textbook, please contact your Longman sales representative.

The Longman Planner. This daily planner for students includes daily, weekly, and monthly calendars, as well as class schedules and a mini-almanac of useful information. It is the perfect accompaniment to a Longman reading or study skills textbook, and is available free to students when shrinkwrapped with this text. 0-321-04573-4.

The Longman Writer's Journal. This journal for writers, free with any Longman English text, offers students a place to think, write, and react. For an examination copy, contact your Longman sales consultant. 0-321-08639-2.

The Longman Researcher's Journal. This journal for writers and researchers, free with this text, helps students plan, schedule, write, and revise their research project. An all-in-one resource for first-time researchers, the journal guides students gently through the research process. 0-321-09530-8.

The Longman Writer's Portfolio. This unique supplement provides students with a space to plan, think about, and present their work. The portfolio includes an assessing/organizing area (including a grammar diagnostic test, a spelling quiz, and project planning worksheets), a before- and during-writing area (including peer review sheets, editing checklists, writing self-evaluations, and a personal editing profile), and an after-writing area (including a progress chart, a final table of contents, and a final assessment). Ask your Longman sales representative for ISBN 0-321-10765-9.

ACKNOWLEDGMENTS

We received invaluable feedback throughout the development of this book from the following reviewers: Kathleen Brennan, Penn State University; Terrence Flaherty, Mankato State University; Stuart Foreman, Millersville University of Pennsylvania; Loretta S. Gray, Central Washington University; Michael Hricik, Westmoreland County Community College; Jill Kelly, Mt. Hood Community College; Daniel Kies, College of DuPage; Vincent McGrath, Mississippi State University; and Richard Moore, Delgado Community College.

We remain indebted to all those people and institutions named in the previous editions, including Kelly Hunt, Francis Christensen, John Mellon, Bill Strong, the English Department at Miami University, and the Exxon Education Foundation. They were our inspiration and support. Dozens of graduate students, colleagues, and friends at Miami and other universities helped us at each step of the way. We'll never forget them. In the current edition, Devin Bustin and Cara Olexa helped by constructing exercises and suggesting changes in chapter narratives.

And, of course, every edition of *The Writer's Options* is indebted to Don Daiker and Andy Kerek, who were there at the birth. Their spirit, imagination, and intelligence live in each page.

THE WRITER'S OPTIONS

PART One

LESSONS IN THE WRITING PROCESS: COMPOSING AND COMBINING

Inventing and Drafting

Preview

The composing process has three phases: invention, drafting, and rewriting. This lesson explores invention and drafting and illustrates three major strategies for discovering ideas: listing, focused freewriting, and the reporter's formula. By considering your readers and your purpose, you can sharpen your focus and decide which details to include and exclude when you begin drafting your paper. If you ask yourself questions about the details you have accumulated, you can create a controlling idea that will hold your writing together. While you select and arrange your ideas, be open to the possibilities offered by the material, because you can usually present the same information in more than one way to suit different purposes.

◆ THE COMPOSING PROCESS

The COMPOSING PROCESS is the series of steps you take to complete a piece of writing. Though no two writers write in exactly the same way, most writers do identify three major steps to their composing process:

- inventing (planning and thinking before you begin drafting)
- drafting (getting your writing down on paper or on a computer screen)
- rewriting (modifying your written draft)

The steps don't always occur in exactly that order. Many writers move back and forth from one to another, from inventing to drafting to more inventing to drafting to rewriting some more, and so on, usually repeating steps as they move through the process.

Most of the lessons in this book discuss the third step in the composing process, rewriting. But before you can rewrite, you obviously need to have a written text in front of you. We've designed this first lesson to help you produce that text; it focuses on invention and drafting.

✍ INVENTION STRATEGIES: DISCOVERING IDEAS

Perhaps the most intimidating aspect of writing is facing an empty page, knowing that you have to fill it with words, sentences, and paragraphs. Where will you get the ideas? How will you find those words? We recommend three strategies that can help you discover ideas: listing, focused freewriting, and the reporter's formula.

Listing

The simplest strategy for discovering ideas is LISTING. Lists can help you (1) collect possible topics, (2) find a suitable topic from among several for an assigned paper, or (3) remember and collect information about that topic.

Listing Topics   One excellent way to generate a list of possible topics is to write quickly without stopping to worry about whether your list is any good: the idea is to make as long a list as you can in five to ten minutes. Be sure to write down every possibility, even those that may initially seem ridiculous. Try to list at least ten items. After you've finished, you can go back over the list and cross out the topics you don't care to write about.

Let's assume your instructor has asked you to write a brief paper on a topic that will require research, either through reading, exploring the Internet, or interviewing knowledgeable people. The first thing you'd want to do is list possible topics, topics you find interesting. Here's one such list:

- assisted suicide
- digital movie making and Hollywood films
- Margaret Sanger and Planned Parenthood
- African American inventors
- the Beatles' influence on rock and roll
- nursing as a career choice for men
- Charles Lindbergh's solo transatlantic flight
- Sir Arthur Conan Doyle and Sherlock Holmes mysteries
- communication among gorillas and chimps
- my grandmother Etta's journey from Poland to Ellis Island

Remember that you'll have great difficulty interesting your readers in any topic that you're not genuinely interested in yourself, so look back over your list and pick a topic that you'd like to learn more about yourself.

Listing to Collect Notes Suppose you included the topic of African American inventors because you wanted to know whether Thomas Edison had any noteworthy rivals who were black. Since you like the topic and want to find out more about it, you do some further reading about it. When you complete your reading, you might find it valuable to compile a new list of what you've learned—just to make sure you don't forget any information or ideas you've run across.

It doesn't matter what this new list of notes looks like. Your goal at this point is to capture any facts, details, or impressions you might use when you select and organize your material. You might list a set of notes like the following about African American inventors:

- Before the Civil War, black inventors in the United States gained little recognition for their work.

- Elijah McCoy invented an automatic lubrication system for steam-operated engines that become so popular it became known as "the real McCoy."

- Garrett Morgan patented the Safety Hood in 1914, a mask that enabled firefighters to enter smoke-filled houses. It was the forerunner of the gas mask.

- When slavery was abolished at the end of the Civil War, blacks gained the right to patent their inventions.

- Garrett Morgan was born in Kentucky in 1875, the child of former slaves.

- Morgan and his brother used the Safety Hood in 1916 to save thirty-two workers trapped by an explosion in a tunnel in the Cleveland Water Works, hundreds of feet below Lake Erie.

- Morgan won the Carnegie Medal and the Medal of Bravery for his rescue.

- The Safety Hood itself won several awards.

- Morgan sold his Safety Hood to fire departments across the country, employing a white man to demonstrate the product when he was in the South.

- Many orders for the Safety Hood were canceled when purchasers learned that Morgan was African American.

- Morgan's other life-saving invention was the traffic signal.

- His invention featured a third signal that halted traffic and allowed pedestrians to cross safely before the next go-signal appeared.

- He invented the signal after witnessing a crash between a horse-drawn carriage and an automobile at a busy crossroad.

- Morgan patented the traffic signal in 1923.

- Morgan's idea became the basis for the red-amber-green three-way signal used in today's traffic lights.
- Morgan's first invention was an accident. Intended for use in reducing friction in high-speed sewing machines, the chemical solution instead developed into GA Morgan Refining Cream, the first hair-straightening lotion.
- Morgan was an early civil rights activist, publishing the *Cleveland Call* in 1920 and serving as treasurer of the Cleveland Association of Colored Men.
- Benjamin Thornton in 1935 invented the first phone-answering message machine.
- W. B. Purvis patented the fountain pen in 1890.
- The first African American woman to receive a patent was Sarah E. Goode, who in 1885 invented a folding cabinet bed, a precursor to today's fold-out sofas.
- Granville Woods patented a number of telephone-telegraph-related inventions, including one that allowed moving trains to stay in contact with railroad stations.
- Woods was denied advancement at the railroad because of his color, so he formed the Woods Railway Telegraph Company in 1884.
- Woods developed the concept of a third rail to power electric trains and subways, just one of the more than fifty patents he received in his lifetime.
- White inventors would take Woods to court for "stealing their ideas," but he won the court battles. One of those white inventors was Thomas Edison.
- After Woods beat Edison twice in court, Edison hired him.
- Woods eventually gained the nickname "The Black Thomas Edison."

At this point, your list probably gives you enough to say to write a detailed short paper. But some people would rather not make lists to discover ideas. If you feel that way, you might try to generate ideas by using another invention strategy—focused freewriting.

Focused Freewriting

FOCUSED FREEWRITING is nonstop writing for a specific period of time: five minutes? ten minutes? until you fill one page or two pages? It's your choice.

Focused freewriting relies upon three guiding principles:

1. Don't stop writing.   During the time you are freewriting, try to write as rapidly as you can without stopping. The technique is called *freewriting* partly because it relies upon "free association." If you "blurt out" whatever pops into your mind, you will probably make some surprising and interesting associations between ideas. But that won't happen if you agonize over what to write next. So just keep writing quickly. If you run into a block and you can't think of what to write next, jot down whatever you are actually thinking ("I'm stumped here. I can't go on. My hand is killing me. My mind is a blank. Should I stop?") until you get back on track with your topic. Or you can simply repeat the last word you've written over and over again (". . . bright sunny smile, smile, smile, smile, smile, smile, smile . . .") until a new idea comes up. Just don't stop your pen from gliding across the page or the cursor from blinking across the screen.

2. Don't edit.   A second reason why the technique is called *freewriting* is that it frees you from the burden of making corrections as you write. When you write, you play two roles: creator and critic. The creator fills up blank pages with new ideas that the critic revises and corrects later. If you let the critic loose too soon, sometimes you paralyze the creator. Have you ever spent two hours on a piece of writing and concluded with a mountain of crumpled-up paper, a monumental headache, and only two sentences of actual writing? That's probably because the critic in you demanded correct, well-thought-out language before the creator in you had produced any language. If you turn off the critic by refusing to edit as you freewrite, you can often avoid that kind of agony. Don't worry about spelling, punctuation, and other usage issues when you're freewriting. The goal is to generate ideas and not to create polished prose. (Later on we'll show you plenty of revising strategies to create polished and correct prose.)

3. Don't stray from the topic.   The reason the technique is called *focused freewriting* is that, unlike an exploratory freewrite when you explore any topic that pops into your mind, this nonstop writing focuses on a specific topic. If you keep focused on your topic, you have a better chance of finding more things to say about it.

Here's the result of five minutes of focused freewriting in which the writer reflects on what she has read in two magazine articles about primate communication:

> *Koko's Kitten*—the book about the gorilla who learned sign language— is fascinating. The author mentions how she made a list in December

for Koko, drawing about twenty pictures of familiar objects such as fruits, vegetables, nuts, dolls, combs, and blankets. Every year Koko hangs up a stocking and gets a lot of presents. According to the author, Koko loves Christmas. Does this make Koko "Christian"? If she is capable of signing abstractions like "love," in what sense is she less than human? Has she a soul? What if she learns the sign for "soul" and claims to have one? Who could deny it to her? Koko's story is about the power of language to create reality. Reality, reality, reality. Now that we know that Koko thinks, she is. "I think, therefore I am" becomes "If I let you know that I think, therefore I am." Francine Patterson wrote an article called "Conversation with a Gorilla" for *National Geographic*. Reading it gave me a better feel for Koko's speech patterns and her 500-word vocabulary. If she uses our language, why isn't she a "person"? When someone asked Koko if she were a person or a gorilla, she answered, "Fine animal gorilla." But what if she had signed, "Person"? On what grounds would she be wrong? I mean, of course, she'd be wrong, but how would we tell her? This fascinates me. I need to read and write more about Koko.

After you finish a focused freewriting, you need to read over what you have written. It's likely that some of it won't be terribly helpful, but you want to look for ideas that surprise you, that interest you, that help you understand your topic more fully. Look for any ideas you feel are important enough to repeat; see if any pattern of ideas has developed. Sometimes one of your ideas can even lead you to another round of focused freewriting; the writer above might freewrite later in order to examine the ethical issues faced by the scientist who experimented on Koko, a thinking being.

Some people believe that freewriting is the single most effective way of generating and discovering material to write about. Others never become comfortable with freewriting. If you feel uncomfortable, you might try a different prewriting strategy—the reporter's formula.

The Reporter's Formula

When you use THE REPORTER'S FORMULA, you ask the questions that newspaper reporters ask in order to generate ideas:

- Who?
- What?
- Where?
- When?
- Why?
- How?

These questions, "the five Ws plus H," help reporters accumulate information about a specific topic. When you ask these six questions, go slowly; spend at least several minutes considering each of them and writing down your responses. Don't worry if the questions seem to overlap. After all, the purpose of the reporter's formula is to generate material; organizing it comes later. Finally, keep in mind that—depending on your topic—some questions are likely to produce more interesting answers than others.

By applying the six questions of the reporter's formula to the topic of Charles Lindbergh's historic transatlantic solo flight, one writer generated the following information, based on her reading:

Who? Charles Lindbergh was a twenty-five-year-old aviator from Minnesota who was born in Detroit. He had flown and navigated mail planes for years and flown from California to New York, making only one stop. He had also been a stunt pilot on the barnstorming circuit. Onlookers thought he was doomed to failure. In fact, his plane was so heavy from the additional fuel it was carrying that it barely cleared the trees at the end of the runway. Lindbergh was viewed as a dark-horse contender to win the transatlantic flying contest.

What? Lindbergh was the first person to fly across the Atlantic Ocean nonstop by himself. His flight took thirty-three hours and covered 3,600 miles as he flew from New York to Paris, France, in a plane capable of 130 miles per hour at its top speed. He carried enough fuel to compensate for an additional 300 miles in case he made a navigational error. He flew at heights ranging from 10 feet above the sea up to 10,000 feet. All he carried in the way of supplies was a bottle of water and five homemade sandwiches (two ham, two beef, and one egg with mayonnaise).

Where? Lindbergh left from Roosevelt Field on Long Island, just outside of New York City. Many years later Roosevelt Field became one of Long Island's first shopping malls. He landed at LeBourget Airport in Paris. After he left Newfoundland behind, he didn't spot land until he came within sight of Ireland, just as he had planned.

When? He left in the morning on May 20, 1927, and landed thirty-three hours later at 10:24 P.M. on May 21 in Paris. Lindbergh's flight preceded the next successful transatlantic flight by approximately two weeks. Clarence Chamberlain and Charles Levine flew nonstop across the Atlantic on June 7 (New York to Berlin).

Why? He set out to win the $25,000 prize offered for the first nonstop flight across the Atlantic. Although he didn't much like the fuss made over him, he was viewed after the flight as a hero. Over 100,000 Parisians greeted him when he landed. Songs were written about him, including one called "Lucky Lindy," a nickname that stuck to him. He became an international hero, receiving the Legion of Honor in Paris two days after his flight and also receiving medals from the kings of Belgium and England.

How? He studied all the planes available, and he chose the Ryan monoplane. He had the plane modified, supervising all the modifications himself. The original wingspan was extended ten feet for more lift. He added stronger landing gear. He increased the fuel capacity from 50 gallons to 450 gallons. He replaced the original seat with a cane chair to save weight, and he installed a 200-horsepower radial air-cooled Wright Whirlwind engine. He had no radio and flew by dead reckoning.

As you can see, the six questions of the reporter's formula can generate a wealth of material, whether it is information you are trying to remember or information you've gathered at the library or on the Internet. Once you've chosen a topic and collected materials for that topic, you can move ahead to the drafting stage where you select and organize the ideas you've generated.

∾ DRAFTING

The Concept of Focus

Which ideas and details you select and how you arrange them depend on your focus. And your focus depends in large part on who will read your draft and for what reason. Imagine yourself in the Arizona desert photographing a giant saguaro cactus with distant purple mountains behind it and your traveling companion standing to the side of it. If you focus tightly on the cactus, the mountains in the background will be out of the picture; your companion may also be cut off the side of the picture. If you use a telephoto lens to focus on the faraway mountains, the cactus and your friend will disappear. If you point the camera directly at your companion, the cactus and the mountains may either become blurred or be shunted aside.

When you sharpen your focus as a writer, something similar happens. You decide which details to include and which to leave out. If you change the focus, your selection of details will also change. When you decide the purpose of your photograph, you can determine whether to focus on the cactus, your friend, or the mountains. If you want the picture to go in your personal photo album as a memento of your trip, you'll probably want your friend clearly focused in the photo; if you want to impress your city-bound friends at home with the immensity of the desert, you may wish to focus on the far-off mountains. If you want to blow up the photo into a poster that will show the unique beauty of the saguaro to anyone who comes into your room, you will zero in on the cactus. When you decide whom you're writing for and the reason you're writing, you can determine which idea to focus on.

Another way to consider focus is to compare it to packing for a trip. As you stand in front of your closet, trying to figure out what to take, you are sure to ask yourself, "Where am I going? Who's going with me? Why are we going?" If you're taking a fishing trip to the lake with your best pals, you're going to pack differently than if you're going to Lake Champlain for a honeymoon, just as you would take different clothes for a business meeting in a cold northern city than you would take for a family vacation trip to a hot, sunny beach. Knowing the situation enables you to pack intelligently, both by including the things you need to take and leaving out the items you won't need.

Finding a Writing Focus

So it is with writing. We might call the focus of a written piece its thesis or its controlling idea. And once you have a clear sense of that thesis, you can include the necessary information and omit what is unnecessary. Sometimes your thesis and even your purpose become clear to you only after you have begun writing. Just as often, what you have written may give you new ideas for developing your draft. Here is a paragraph you might have written to support the thesis that Lindbergh was a skillful planner and pilot:

> When twenty-five-year-old Charles Lindbergh took off from Long Island to claim the $25,000 prize for flying nonstop to Paris, most of the onlookers thought he was just another ex-barnstormer doomed to failure. They didn't know that **"Lucky Lindy" was a skillful planner and pilot.** He had carefully chosen the Ryan monoplane and supervised its modification. He had installed a 200-horsepower radial air-cooled engine that gave him a top speed of 130 miles per hour. He had the wingspan extended by ten feet for more lift. And he had the normal 50-gallon fuel tank increased to 450 gallons. He was an excellent navigator and pilot who kept track of wind direction and wind speed by flying ten feet above the ocean. When he sighted land, it was precisely where he expected—in Ireland.

But after completing this first draft, you might begin to see a new idea emerging—the contrast between the nickname "Lucky Lindy" and the facts indicating that Lindbergh had prepared for his flight with great care and skill. You also consider that your classmates may not know very much about Lindbergh at all, but that nickname may sound familiar, so you might decide to focus on it. To develop this contrast as the controlling idea of a revised version of your draft, you would first want to return to your notes for additional supporting information. There you would find two further details to illustrate how carefully Lindbergh had prepared. He was an experienced pilot of barnstormers and mail planes, and he was carrying enough fuel for a 300-mile navigational error. By incorporating these details and excluding others, by revising and rearranging sentences, and especially by emphasizing in both your first and last sentences the contrast between luck on one hand and care and skill on the other, you are now able to construct a draft with a different focus:

> **Though the world called him "Lucky Lindy"** after he became the first person to fly nonstop across the Atlantic, twenty-five-year-old **Charles Lindbergh had actually depended on skill and careful preparation** for the flight. He was an expert pilot and navigator with years of experience flying barnstormers and mail planes. He carefully selected the Ryan monoplane from among the available aircraft as the best suited for his difficult task. And he personally supervised its modification, which included extending its wingspan by ten feet and increasing its fuel capacity by 400 gallons in order to allow for a 300-mile navigational error. When "Lucky Lindy" touched down in Paris thirty-three hours after leaving Long Island, it was because he had left little to luck.

Asking Yourself Questions

Sometimes you can have difficulty finding a controlling idea; one approach, already illustrated, is to freewrite in order to discover what you really want to say. Another helpful approach is to ask questions about the information you've gathered. Perhaps you decide that your readers, the members of your peer editing group, probably don't know very much about Lindbergh's historic flight and that your primary purpose in writing about it will be to help them appreciate Lindbergh's great accomplishment. So you ask yourself, "How was Lindbergh able to complete this amazing feat and make history?" Your answer to that question, that he succeeded because of his knowledge, experience, thoroughness, and luck, will become your controlling idea. The controlling idea allows you to judge which details to include. That Lindbergh had no radio and that he took along five sandwiches are not clearly connected to the reasons for his success. In the same way, the facts that the flight took thirty-three hours, that it began at Roosevelt Field, or that it won Lindbergh $25,000 are not directly related to knowledge, experience, thoroughness, and luck. Because you omit such irrelevant material and include only details that develop the controlling idea, you construct a unified, sharply focused draft:

> **Charles Lindbergh was successful in being the first to fly nonstop across the Atlantic because of his knowledge, his experience, his thoroughness, and his luck.** He knew airplanes as both a pilot and a navigator. He had gained extensive flying experience from mail runs and the barnstorming circuit. He carefully selected his own plane and thor-

oughly modified it for the arduous flight by extending its wingspan, installing stronger landing gear, and increasing its fuel capacity. And his timing was lucky, since the next nonstop flight across the Atlantic took place within two weeks of his journey.

However, the same set of notes might lead you in a different direction. Perhaps you noticed that some of your notes emphasize that Lindbergh quickly was hailed as a hero after his flight. Since you can often make your point by relating it to what your audience knows, you might ask, "How did Lindbergh's heroics differ from the heroics of today's multimillionaire athletes?" Your next step is to select from your notes those details that are relevant and discard those that are not. The most relevant details for convincing your readers of Lindbergh's heroism relate to the length and difficulty of his journey, to his primitive flight instruments, and to the uniqueness of his achievement. Those details might be organized into a draft like this:

While today's wealthy basketball stars become "heroes" instantly by signing multimillion-dollar contracts to dunk a basketball, Charles Lindbergh earned his status as a hero when he landed safely in Paris in 1927 after flying nonstop across the Atlantic, a feat no one had done before. And he did it under almost impossible conditions. He piloted a single-engine Ryan monoplane capable of flying no faster than 130 miles per hour. He flew alone for thirty-three hours, without a radio and with only a sextant and magnetic compass for navigational help. He often cruised but ten feet above the ocean waves to estimate wind speed and wind direction. Because his was truly a heroic feat, **Lindbergh deserved to be considered a hero in 1927—and even now, more than seventy-five years later.**

Notice that your controlling idea helped to determine which details to keep and which to omit. You didn't need the facts about knowledge, experience, thoroughness, and luck to support the controlling idea that "Lindbergh deserved to be considered a hero in 1927—and even now, more than seventy-five years later."

Perhaps your instructor's assignment asked you to examine how technology contributed to a historic event. In that case, your purpose would be different: you would try to show your reader (your instructor) how Lindbergh used technology to achieve his great success. Now your question is likely to be "How did Lindbergh modify his plane?" rather than "How was Lindbergh able to complete this successful feat?" or "Did he deserve to be treated as a hero?" By focusing on the details about the plane's wingspan, landing gear, engine, fuel capacity, and seat, you might write a draft developing the idea that after Lindbergh modified the plane, even its manufacturers wouldn't have recognized it:

The plane Charles Lindbergh flew nonstop across the Atlantic began as a Ryan monoplane. That was before Lindbergh started modifying it. First, he extended the wingspan by ten feet and added stronger landing gear. Then he increased its fuel capacity from 50 to 450 gallons and installed a 200-horsepower Wright Whirlwind engine. Before he was through, he had even replaced the original seat with a lightweight cane chair. **When he was done, the original builders probably wouldn't have recognized their own creation.**

Once again, you used the controlling idea to govern the selection of facts, leaving out the details of Lindbergh's difficult flight and primitive instruments.

Developing a Full-Length Draft

These various Charles Lindbergh drafts illustrate an important principle of drafting: It is almost always possible to use the same information in different ways to accomplish a variety of purposes. All of the different versions have their roots in the same details generated about Lindbergh's flight; how you select and arrange those details depends on what your thesis is going to be, who is going to read your draft, and what you want them to get out of it.

You can use the same process to create a full-length essay or research report as you do to create a paragraph. To expand the last paragraph into a longer paper, for example, you could explore Lindbergh's modifications of the Ryan monoplane in much greater detail, devoting a page or more to each modification. But whether your draft is one page or ten, you need to carefully select and organize your ideas—according to the purpose and focus on your paper and the demands of your readers.

EXERCISES

Try the following exercises for some practice in developing a controlling idea and in using details to construct a focused and specific paragraph.

Selecting and Arranging Ideas

Mount Rushmore

Construct a unified and ordered paragraph by picking one of the three statements below to serve as a controlling idea and then choosing appropriate supporting details from the notes. Consider your readers: Will they be sympathetic or unsympathetic to your position?

A. Some Americans view Mount Rushmore as a priceless American tribute to national ideals.

B. Some Americans view Mount Rushmore as a symbol of some disturbing aspects of American life.

C. Creating and repairing the Mount Rushmore monument illustrate how difficult it is to overcome natural forces.

1. Mount Rushmore is the world's largest piece of sculpture.

2. The Black Hills are sacred land to the Sioux.

3. Doane Robinson wanted a permanent tourist attraction for South Dakota.

4. Robinson (1924) suggested a "colossal monument" of Buffalo Bill or Chief Red Cloud.

5. John Gutzon de la Mothe Borglum was chosen to be the sculptor.

6. Borglum had worked on a quarter-mile-long bas-relief of Confederate soldiers at Stone Mountain, Georgia.

7. Borglum argued with the Stone Mountain planning group, destroyed his work, and fled Georgia before he could be arrested.

8. Mount Rushmore has a near-vertical granite wall 500 feet long and 400 feet high.

9. Sioux Indians claim the land on which Mount Rushmore is built.

10. The workers had to build a staircase of 504 wooden steps on forty-five inclined ramps to get to the top.

11. The first step in repairing Mount Rushmore was to take hundreds of aerial photographs in order to define the monument's structural features.

12. Structural cracks were overlaid on the computer model to indicate where the repair work should begin.

13. Borglum initially carved Jefferson's face on Washington's right but then carved it again on the left.

14. The monument needed repairs by 1991.

15. The repairs cost $40 million.

16. The repair company used a computer model to produce a three-dimensional image of Mount Rushmore.

17. It took Borglum fourteen years to carve the four faces.

18. Borglum was a Ku Klux Klan supporter and an active anti-Semite.

19. Borglum proposed Presidents Washington, Jefferson, Lincoln, and Theodore Roosevelt instead of Wild West figures.

20. Borglum wanted to memorialize four great national leaders.

21. Native Americans feel that the four presidents "committed acts of atrocity against our people." (Quoted from Tim Giago, Oglala Sioux spokesperson.)

22. Borglum's workers had to build a new road to get to Mount Rushmore.

23. Within 500 generations, the monument will erode to the point where the presidents look like bald little children.

24. Sioux Indian land claims date back to 1868.

25. In 1980, the U.S. Supreme Court ruled in favor of the Sioux and ordered the U.S. government to pay $263 million in fines and interest.

26. The Sioux have refused the money, which sits in a trust account; they want their land back.

27. Funding for the monument kept running out, but Borglum convinced Calvin Coolidge and Franklin Roosevelt to use government money to finish it.

28. The Rushmore granite is eroding at a rate of one inch per 10,000 years.

African American Inventors

Using the details generated in the example on pages 5–6, construct a unified and ordered paragraph that explains how the history of African American inventors is a story of ingenuity overcoming racism. Consider your readers: Will they be sympathetic or unsympathetic to your position?

The Personal and the Public

Each of you is an individual with unique personal experiences to remember and write about. However, each of you lives in a public world as well, the world of school and work and community. Personal lives, then, always take place against the public background of larger events. Read the exercises below. Each provides a list of ideas and details about a public world in which you live. Pick one of the four topics and follow the instructions on writing an essay that combines your personal experiences with the information you have learned.

1. **Entertainment**: Read "A Fair to Remember" (Lesson 7, pp. 105–107) about the famous Chicago World's Fair and "Eat and Run" (Lesson 4, pp. 55–56) about the very first McDonald's restaurant. These two exercises provide a list of ideas and details that explore the history of two of the more popular current forms of entertainment: amusement parks and dating at fast-food restaurants. Write an essay about either your favorite amusement park or your favorite fast-food place to go on a date. Try to weave into your essay some of the history you have learned from the sentence-combining exercise you have read, contrasting past and present, or explaining how things have remained the same.

2. **Environmental Issues**: Read "Saving the Forests, Saving Ourselves" (Lesson 9, pp. 135–136) and "No More Burgers" (Lesson 8, pp. 123–124). These two exercises focus on the environment: the first describes the destruction of the world's rain forests and the second explains the consequences of our culture's reliance on beef as a source of food. A famous slogan of environmentalists is "Think globally. Act locally." Write an essay about a local environmental issue in your community: are local developers destroying wetlands to build new homes? is the local government adequately protecting the natural environment in your area? is there a garbage dump or an industrial waste site in the area? As you write your essay, be sure to include your own personal experiences and weave into the paper some of the ideas and details from the sentence-combining exercises, giving the global context of environmental issues that our society faces.

3. **Surviving Persecution**: Read "Trail of Tears" (Lesson 9, pp. 137–138) and "Underground Railroad" (Lesson 4, pp. 57–58). The first exercise lists ideas and details about the tragic forced relocation of the Cherokees from their traditional homeland; the second exercise explains how escaped

slaves from the American South made it to freedom up North. Has your family experienced persecution in the past because of your race or ethnic origins? How did they find their way to where you live today? Tell your family's personal story of relocation or flight; be sure to weave into that story some details from either "Trail of Tears" or "Underground Railroad."

4. **Immigrating to the "New World"**: Read "Ellis Island: Dream and Nightmare" (Lesson 3, pp. 44–45) and "Angel Island: A Story Worth Preserving" (Lesson 11, pp. 170–171). These exercises list ideas and details about European and Asian immigration to the United States a century ago. If your family immigrated to this country, tell the story of that journey, using information from the sentence-combining exercises to provide some historical background to your narrative.

Playing with Sentences

Preview

We believe you can learn how to write interesting sentences and to employ effective writing strategies when you play with sentences and writing in nonthreatening exercises. So this first lesson gives you the opportunity to play, no holds barred. Its major goal is to let you see that sentence combining can be fun and productive—and that even without instructions to produce specific structures or strategies, you can do well.

❧ PLAYING WITH SENTENCES

Basketball players have a number of moves they use as situations change in a game. Experienced players know how to choose among the moves according to the time remaining on the clock, the defensive alignment, the positions of their teammates, or the number of fouls they've accrued. If Kobe Bryant receives the ball near the foul line, he might shoot, drive left, drive right, pass off, or call for a time-out. Because they practice lots of different moves, experienced players have more options and are more apt to choose successful moves than are inexperienced players.

The same is true of writers. Experienced writers have a number of moves they use as situations change in their writing. If J. K. Rowling is explaining a point, she might use relative clauses and appositives in her sentences. If she's giving narrative details, she might use participles and absolute phrases. If she wants to produce a formal argument, she might use balanced phrases, like Winston Churchill's "blood, sweat, and tears," or repetition, like Franklin Roosevelt's, "The only thing we have to fear is fear itself." Like experienced athletes, experienced writers practice lots of different moves, so they have more options and are more apt to choose successful strategies than are inexperienced writers. James Joyce, the great Irish novelist, recognized that a writer has lots of language options to choose from. He once commented on his writing practice, "What I am seeking is the perfect order of words in the sentence. You can see for yourself how many different ways they might be arranged."

One major aim of this book is to help you develop a series of useful structures and strategies and to suggest ways of choosing among them in specific situations, particularly at the drafting and revising stages of your writing. Using a variety of structures and strategies will help you write papers your readers will consider both interesting and readable. Readers will understand that you're aiming to make your writing as effective as possible. They will see you as a writer who knows how to control sentence structure, a writer who produces sophisticated prose.

The way we go about teaching these structures and strategies is through sentence-combining exercises. They're simple exercises that will come naturally to you and may even prove to be fun. We hope so. Here's an example. If you were given the two sentences

It surprised me.

Jane arrived late.

and told to put them together into a single sentence in as many ways as you could, you might begin your list with the following sentences:

It surprised me that Jane arrived late.

I was surprised when Jane arrived late.

Jane's late arrival surprised me.

What surprised me was the lateness of Jane's arrival.

Because Jane arrived late, I was surprised.

Jane arrived late, surprising me.

You get the idea. You can think of lots of other single sentences to make with the original pair: there are at least 500.

In this book, we try to give you lots of opportunities to play with sentences, to practice various options for creating them, like basketball players practicing different moves on the court. We'll give you exercises that allow you to practice creating structures like relative clauses, participial phrases, and absolutes, as well as strategies like coherence, repetition, and subordination. Don't be thrown off by the names for the structures and strategies, any more than a young basketball player is thrown off by the names of the moves. You probably know how to create most of them already, whether you know their names or not. But you might not have used these structures and strategies enough in your own writing to know exactly when or where they will do you the most good.

The basic principle behind the book is that you have lots of different ways to write sentences and to put them together into larger units like paragraphs and essays. But some ways of putting sentences together are more effective than others, given the outcome you are after. You want to learn how to exercise your options and to select from among them so that your reader will recognize your writing as clear, strong, and focused. We believe that by playing with sentences and paragraphs, especially when you rewrite, you'll learn how to use the structures and strategies effectively. In his book *On Writing,* Stephen King says that "writing is at its best—always, always, always—when it is a kind of inspired play for the writer."

We placed this chapter after the lesson on drafting to emphasize the fact that much of what we present in this book presumes that you have something already written in front of you when you begin combining sentences. In that sense, sentence combining is one way of practicing how to revise your prose.

As the combining exercise about Jane arriving late indicates, there are no "right answers." Each new version might be used effectively in certain situations. Each might be inappropriate in others. When you play with them, try out different sentences, and discuss them in class, you'll learn which sentence, or set of sentences, will produce the effect you want in any given situation. Suppose, for instance, that you combine Sentences 8–11 in "Deluxe Pizza" (pp. 25–26) like this:

8. The sauce steams.

9. The sauce bubbles.

10. Its smell fills the room.

11. The smell is slightly sweet.

↓

The sauce steams and bubbles and fills the room with a slightly sweet smell.

Nothing wrong with that. Because it compounds the verbs, it makes the actions **steam, bubble,** and **fill** equivalent. Perhaps after writing this sentence, you decide that you don't want to make all the actions equivalent, that you'd rather emphasize one of them. If you revise **fill** into an **-ing** form, you make that verb different from the other two, emphasizing it:

The sauce steams and bubbles, **filling the room with a slightly sweet smell.**

If you decide to emphasize the appearance of the sauce, you might revise both **steam** and **bubble** into **-ing** forms and begin the sentence with them, as in

Steaming and bubbling, the sauce fills the room with its slightly sweet smell.

Or you might decide to focus your reader's attention even more emphatically on what the sauce looks like by separating **steaming** and **bubbling** from the predicate of the sentence:

> The sauce—**steaming and bubbling**—fills the room with its slightly sweet smell.

The point is that you have lots of options. Experienced writers, like experienced basketball players, understand when to use this move or that, according to the situation at hand.

Since there are no right answers, you do the exercises in this book correctly when you use them to practice the different ways you can compose and revise sentences and paragraphs. But unless you remember to transfer them into your own writing, the lessons you learn from this book are useless. Practicing and making choices among the options and then transferring what you learn to your own writing will help you become a better writer.

Most lessons in this book are built around one specific structure or strategy. The lessons move from prewriting and drafting strategies to sentence structures useful for revising to strategies concerned with how to revise paragraphs to achieve certain effects. You can follow our order through the book or pick and choose from the lessons as you or your instructor sees fit.

This lesson is not built around a specific structure or strategy; it is simply a set of exercises that allow you to practice combining sentences. We hope that by working on the sentences and paragraphs in this unit, you will see that sentence combining is not threatening. You can do it and do it well.

Have fun working through the book. Make your playing useful, and learn a lot about writing by doing the exercises. Most important, don't forget to apply the lessons to your own writing.

EXERCISES

Playing First

You can revise the following sentences into a paragraph that explores Jackie Robinson's accomplishments. The spaces between the groups of sentences indicate possible sentence boundaries, but you may ignore the boundaries whenever you want to make your sentences longer or shorter. Don't forget to play with the sentences. Try different versions for different effects.

1. Jackie Robinson became the first black man to play major-league baseball.
2. This happened in 1947.

3. Robinson faced severe racial prejudice.
4. The prejudice was from fans.
5. And the prejudice was from players.
6. This happened during that first season.

7. And he received several threatening letters.
8. He kept playing, though.

9. He played first base for the Brooklyn Dodgers.
10. He had never been a first baseman before.

11. He had stolen twenty-nine bases.
12. He had batted .297.
13. And he had won the first-ever Rookie of the Year award.
14. All this happened by the end of the season.

15. Eventually, he was inducted into the Baseball Hall of Fame.

16. But more important, he helped to break the barrier.
17. The barrier had kept black athletes out of professional sports.

Left Out

You can revise the following sentences into a paragraph on the plight of left-handers in society. You may add details if you wish to make the paragraph more vivid and personal. Don't forget to play with the sentences. Try different versions for different effects.

1. Life is difficult.
2. This is true for left-handers.

3. They live in a world.
4. Everything is made for righties in the world.
5. Can openers are made for righties.
6. Scissors are made for righties.
7. School desks are made for righties.

8. Teachers often force lefties to write right-handed.
9. Coaches often force them to play right-handed.

10. Even the word for "left" makes lefties outsiders.
11. This is true in most languages.

12. *Lyft* meant weak and useless.
13. This was in Old English.

14. *Links* means clumsy or awkward.
15. This is in German.

16. *Gauche* means ugly or uncouth.
17. This is in French.

18. But things may be changing because of [this].
19. Left-handers are organizing.
20. Left-handers are fighting for recognition.

21. Recently, they declared International Left-Handers Day.
22. It is on August 13.

23. If [this happens], then [this happens].

24. Left-handers win their "rights."

25. Southpaws won't be left out anymore.

Rock and Roll Together

You can revise the following sentences into a paragraph that explains the roots of rock and roll. Don't forget to play with the sentences. Try different versions for different effects.

1. Clint Black, Bob Dylan, Toad the Wet Sprocket, and Tina Turner have something in common.

2. What is it?

3. Their music has its roots in the old murder ballads of poor southern whites.

4. Their music has its roots in the raw dance tunes of poor southern whites.

5. Their music has its roots in the blues of poor blacks.

6. Their music has its roots in the hollers of poor blacks.

7. Their music has its roots in the sung sermons of poor blacks.

8. Black rhythm and blues and white country-western merged.

9. They merged in such figures as Elvis Presley and Chuck Berry.

10. This happened in the 1950s.

11. Together, blacks and whites created rock and roll.

12. Rock and roll was a new music.

13. The new music was filled with power and mystery.

Deluxe Pizza

Revise the following sentences into a description of an appetizing pizza. If you choose, you may add details to make the description more vivid. Don't forget to play with the sentences. Try different versions for different effects.

1. The pizza sits in the middle of the table.

2. It is fresh from the oven.

3. Its crust rises up.

4. The crust is thick.

5. The crust is golden brown.

6. It is like a wall.

7. The wall surrounds the rest of the ingredients.

8. The sauce steams.

9. The sauce bubbles.

10. Its smell fills the room.

11. The smell is slightly sweet.

12. The pizza is covered with pepperoni slices.

13. They are shiny.

14. They are dappled.

15. They contrast with the sauce.

16. The sauce is dull red.

17. Mushroom slices rest in the sauce.

18. The slices are shriveled.

19. The slices are soft.

20. Their edges are slightly curved.

21. Green olives are scattered about.

22. Black olives are scattered about.

23. They dot the surface.

24. Creamy cheese melts over the pizza.

25. It enmeshes everything in its weblike strands.

26. The strands trap the taste until someone releases it with a bite.

Soar like a Hawk; Land like a Coyote

Revise the following sentences into a paragraph on how to fly a hang glider. Add details if you wish to make the paragraph more vivid and personal. Don't forget to play with the sentences. Try different versions for different effects.

1. Suppose you'd like to soar through the sky like a hawk.

2. Then try hang gliding.

3. To fly a hang glider, you [do this].
4. Hang in a harness under a parachute-like wing.
5. You steer with an aluminum control bar.

6. To get airborne, you have to [do this].
7. You run down a steep slope and jump into the air.

8. Then you must stay afloat.
9. You ride air currents to stay afloat.
10. You soar and dip like a seagull or a hawk.

11. You shift your weight to the right or left.
12. You can change the glider's direction.

13. Flying is fun.
14. Landings are often rough.

15. You land with a simple move.
16. You push the control bar up to stall the glider.

17. And that sometimes sends pilots [doing this].
18. They smash into ground obstacles.

19. So you can soar like a hawk.
20. You can crash to earth like Wile E. Coyote.

Pro Athletes

Revise the following sentences into a paragraph on women gladiators. Don't forget to play with the sentences. Try different versions for different effects.

1. She is grabbing rebounds.
2. And she is blocking shots.
3. Lisa Leslie fits our picture of the professional woman athlete.
4. She is the tall, aggressive center for the Los Angeles Sparks.

5. We imagine [this].
6. Women have become professional athletes only in contemporary times.

7. But women were professional athletes as early as biblical times.

8. Archaeologists and historians have found evidence.

9. Women even fought as gladiators.

10. Gladiators are the ultimate professional athletes.

11. They were competing for money and their lives.

12. Archaeologists have unearthed a stone carving.

13. The carving shows two women gladiators.

14. They are opposite one another.

15. They are armed with swords and crouching behind shields.

16. The archaeologists unearthed the stone near a Roman amphitheater on the outskirts of London.

17. Several Roman writers tell of women gladiators in the arena.

18. They were parrying and thrusting with their heavy swords.

19. They finally succumbed to the bloody strikes.

20. But the inscription on the back of the stone carving says [this].

21. Amazonia and Achilia were allowed to walk free from the arena.

22. This was as a reward for their fighting ability.

23. Real pros!

PART *Two*

LESSONS IN STYLE: REVISING SENTENCES

Relative Clauses

Preview

This lesson explains how you can construct a relative clause by replacing a noun or noun phrase with a pronoun like **which, that, who, whom,** or **whose,** according to whether the noun refers to a human or a thing or whether it is possessive. You will learn how you can use relative clauses to clear up relationships, to make your writing more concise, to control the emphasis of your sentences, and to help you develop paragraphs.

✧ CONSTRUCTING RELATIVE CLAUSES

One strategy you can use to revise your writing is called the RELATIVE CLAUSE. It can help you write more economical sentences and control focus in your paragraphs. You construct a relative clause by replacing a noun or noun phrase with a pronoun like **which, that, who, whom,** or **whose.** For example, if you replace the repeated noun phrase "the spear-throwing device" with the relative pronoun **which,** you can make the following two sentences into a single sentence with a relative clause:

> The Cro-Magnons developed a spear-throwing device. ~~The spear-throwing device~~ improved the range of their weapons by thirty yards.

↓

> The Cro-Magnons developed a spear-throwing device **which** improved the range of their weapons by thirty yards.

When you construct a relative clause, you place one sentence into another, as you might place a small box within a large box. Let's take a closer look at how to do it. The second sentence below repeats the noun **motorists.**

> In many states motorists can have their driver's licenses suspended. The motorists have received three or more speeding tickets.

If you replace such a repeated word or phrase with a relative pronoun such as **who,** you produce a relative clause:

who
~~The motorists~~ have received three or more speeding tickets.

Then you can place the new relative clause within the other sentence, as you would put a little box within a bigger box:

> In many states motorists who have received three or more speeding tickets can have their driver's license suspended.

✂ CHOOSING RELATIVE PRONOUNS

You replace a noun according to two criteria: whether the noun refers to a human or whether it is a subject or object. If the relative pronoun replaces a subject noun that refers to things, like "the sign language" in the following example, you can select either **that** or **which** to introduce the relative clause:

To communicate between tribes, the Native Americans of the Great Plains used an intricate sign language. ~~The sign language~~ contained a series of mutually understood gestures.

To communicate between tribes, the Native Americans of the Great Plains used an intricate sign language **that contained a series of mutually understood gestures.**

OR

To communicate between tribes, the Native Americans of the Great Plains used an intricate sign language **which contained a series of mutually understood gestures.**

If, on the other hand, the relative pronoun replaces a subject noun phrase that refers to people, then you can select either **who** or **that:**

The peasant farmers still work in the ancient ways of their ancestors. ~~The peasant farmers~~ till the Nile Delta.

The peasant farmers **who till the Nile Delta** still work in the ancient ways of their ancestors.

OR

The peasant farmers **that till the Nile Delta** still work in the ancient ways of their ancestors.

When you replace an object noun phrase that refers to people, you have three choices: **whom, that,** or no pronoun at all. Since **whom** sounds more formal, many writers choose **that** or no pronoun at all:

> The players had won the first Women's World Cup soccer championship. The President invited ~~the players~~ to the White House.

> The players **whom the President invited to the White House** had won the first Women's World Cup soccer championship.
>
> OR
>
> The players **that the President invited to the White House** had won the first Women's World Cup soccer championship.
>
> OR
>
> The players **the President invited to the White House** had won the first Women's World Cup soccer championship.

When you replace a possessive noun or possessive pronoun to make a relative clause, you use **whose:**

> John Grisham did not plan to become a writer but trained instead as a lawyer. ~~His~~ lawyer novels made him the best-selling author of the 1990s, with over 60 million books sold.

> John Grisham, whose lawyer novels made him the best-selling author of the 1990s, with over 60 million books sold, did not plan to become a writer but trained instead as a lawyer.

✃ RELATIVE CLAUSES WITH PREPOSITIONS OR EXPRESSIONS OF QUANTITY

You can construct a relative clause to follow a preposition like **to, for, of, with, by,** or **in:**

> Aesop's fables are famous for the moral lessons they teach. In ~~Aesop's fables~~ animals act like human beings.

> Aesop's fables, **in which animals act like human beings,** are famous for the moral lessons they teach.

The Strange Case of Mrs. Hudson's Cat is a book. An updated Sherlock Holmes solves complicated physics problems ~~in the book.~~

↓

The Strange Case of Mrs. Hudson's Cat is a book **in which an updated Sherlock Holmes solves complicated physics problems.**

You can also construct a relative clause from a sentence that begins with a phrase which expresses quantity, like **many of, some of, none of, several of,** or **all of:**

The impressionist painters tried to present objects not as they are but as they appear to the eye. Most of ~~the impressionist painters~~ rejected photographic realism.

↓

The impressionist painters, **most of whom rejected photographic realism,** tried to present objects not as they are but as they appear to the eye.

Relative clauses are easy to construct from various sentence patterns, and they're useful in a number of different ways, as you'll see in the following sections.

ꝭ PUNCTUATING RELATIVE CLAUSES

Sometimes you have to choose whether to use commas to separate a relative clause from the rest of the sentence. You choose according to how the clause relates to the meaning of the sentence. The first sentence below, with a comma, means something very different from the identically worded sentence without a comma. If you read them out loud, pausing at the comma, you should be able to hear the difference in their meaning:

The parents and teachers of our school decided against history books, **which ignore the accomplishments of minorities.**

The parents and teachers of our school decided against history books **which ignore the accomplishments of minorities.**

The sentence with the comma makes two statements: (1) parents and teachers decided against history books and (2) ALL history books ignore the accomplishments of minorities. The sentence without the comma makes a single statement: teachers and parents decided against only those history books which ignore the accomplishments of minorities.

When you use a relative clause without commas, you are saying that the information in the clause is true of only some of the things or people you mentioned in the sentence (some history books ignore the accomplishments of minorities, while other history books do not). When you use a relative clause with commas, you are saying the information in the clause is true of all the things or people mentioned in the sentence (history books, all of them, ignore the accomplishments of minorities). Another important characteristic of a relative clause with commas is that it does not allow you to use **that** as the relative pronoun or to drop an object noun phrase. You must use **who, whom,** or **which.**

✍ USING RELATIVE CLAUSES FOR EMPHASIS AND ECONOMY

When two sentences sit next to one another, sometimes it's unclear which is the main idea. For instance, in the following two sentences, readers can't tell which idea is more important:

> A wealthy graduate had offered to donate $500,000 to Garland University's general fund. The university asked the wealthy graduate to contribute directly to the athletic program.

But if you make one or the other sentence into a relative clause when you revise, readers will understand that the idea in the clause is not as important as the idea in the sentence:

> The university asked the wealthy graduate, **who had offered to donate $500,000 to Garland University's general fund,** to contribute directly to the athletic program.

Because the information in a relative clause normally adds to and comments upon the information in a main clause, relative clauses can help you control what you emphasize in your sentences. You normally place the most important information into a main clause, the less important information into a relative clause. When the next two example sentences appear beside one another, the ideas in them are essentially equivalent in weight. By revising the second into a relative clause, you are claiming that the fact about homeopathic physicians and chiropractors being distrusted by medical doctors is the important point and that the fact that they treat illnesses with natural remedies is less important:

> Chiropractors and homeopathic physicians are distrusted by medical doctors. Chiropractors and homeopathic physicians treat patients with natural remedies instead of drugs.

> Chiropractors and homeopathic physicians—**who treat patients with natural remedies instead of drugs**—are distrusted by medical doctors.

In contrast, if you make the first sentence into a relative clause and keep the second as the main clause, as in the example below, you focus on the fact that homeopathic physicians and chiropractors treat patients with natural remedies, and you deemphasize the fact that they are distrusted by medical doctors:

> Chiropractors and homeopathic physicians, **who are distrusted by medical doctors,** treat patients with natural remedies instead of drugs.

Not only do relative clauses allow you to write more focused sentences, but they also allow you to write more economically. The sentences with relative clauses are three words shorter than the two original sentences, and they both eliminate the distracting repetition of the phrase "chiropractors and homeopathic physicians."

✐ RELATIVE CLAUSES AND PARAGRAPH DEVELOPMENT

The focus of any sentence generally determines the content of the sentence that follows it. You would expect a paragraph with the first example about chiropractors and homeopathic physicians to continue in the following manner, making a comment about medical doctors and their view of alternative approaches:

> Chiropractors and homeopathic physicians—**who treat patients with natural remedies instead of drugs**—are distrusted by medical doctors. Doctors claim that such practitioners of alternative medicine don't substantiate their treatment methods through "scientific" experiments.

You would also expect a paragraph with the second example to continue by expanding the idea that homeopathic physicians and chiropractors treat illnesses with natural remedies, as in the following, which tells why they use natural remedies:

> Chiropractors and homeopathic physicians, **who are distrusted by medical doctors,** treat patients with natural remedies instead of drugs. Practitioners of alternative medicine claim to enhance the body's natural healing ability; they claim to treat the cause of a disease, not its symptoms.

It is important to remember that sentence structure affects the development of paragraphs as well as the look and feel of sentences. The way you construct sentences can enhance paragraph development or detract from it. Sometimes all you have to do to further the development of a paragraph is to turn one sentence into a relative clause and combine it with another sentence. The following paragraph, for instance, emphasizes the adaptability of the Norway rat; that is the point of the first and last sentences. But the second sentence, because it states how the rat reached North America, shifts the focus from the main point and disrupts the continuity of the paragraph:

> The Norway rat is regarded by experts as the most destructive mammal on earth and the most adaptive to changing situations and environments. The Norway rat actually reached this country on the ships of many nations. It abounds in the debris of North American cities, resisting all attempts to control it.

If you convert the second sentence into a relative clause, you can lessen its importance and keep the paragraph focused on its central point—the rat's adaptability:

> The Norway rat, **which actually reached this country on the ships of many nations,** is regarded by experts as the most destructive mammal on earth and the most adaptive to changing situations and environments. It abounds in the debris of North American cities, resisting all attempts to control it.

❧ PLAYING WITH RELATIVE CLAUSES

In the next few pages, you'll have an opportunity to play with relative clauses, constructing them, moving them around, and using them to write economically and to focus your sentences and paragraphs. When you're drafting or revising your own papers, remember to look for opportunities to use relative clauses. They can make your writing more concise, better focused, and more fully developed.

EXERCISES

Constructing Relative Clauses

I. Revise each sequence below into a single sentence by converting the marked sentence into a relative clause. Decide whether the clause needs to be separated from the rest of the sentence by a comma.

EXAMPLE

1. A weak economy can cloud the job prospects of college graduates.
2. A weak economy discourages older workers from retiring.

A weak economy **that discourages older workers from retiring** can cloud the job prospects of college graduates.

A. **1.** Paleontologists were excited to discover the fossil of a feathered dinosaur in Mongolia.

   2. Paleontologists believe birds are descended from dinosaurs.

B. **1.** Dogs often pick up some very bad habits.

   2. Dogs copy the behavior of their owners.

C. **1.** The Chinese eat a diet.

   2. The diet contains one-third less fat than the American diet.

D. **1.** Fishermen off the coast of Alaska can now fax the Domino's in Juneau for a pizza delivery to their boats in the Bering Sea.

   2. Fishermen off the coast of Alaska work up an appetite for more than tuna casserole.

E. **1.** El Niño can cause droughts in Australia and flooding rains in North America.

   2. El Niño begins with an unusual shift in the southwest Pacific wind.

   3. The shift in the southwest Pacific wind changes ocean currents.

38

II. Revise each sequence below into a single sentence by converting one or more of the original sentences into a relative clause. If the sentences allow, write more than one version for each sequence. And decide whether the clause needs to be separated from the sentence by commas.

EXAMPLE

1. Huntington, Long Island, was once praised by Whitman for its natural beauty.

2. Huntington, Long Island, is now the site of an ugly sprawling megamall.

Huntington, Long Island, **which is now the site of an ugly sprawling megamall,** was once praised by Whitman for its natural beauty.

OR

Huntington, Long Island, **which was once praised by Whitman for its natural beauty,** is now the site of an ugly sprawling megamall.

F. **1.** Groups concerned with family values sent e-mail petitions to the video game manufacturer of *Panty Raider*, objecting to the depiction of women as sex toys and men as violent.

   2. Groups concerned with family values denied that they are humorless censors.

G. **1.** Bold and beautiful, Mata Hari is the most renowned female spy in history.

   2. Mata Hari insolently blew a kiss to the firing squad that executed her.

H. **1.** J. K. Rowling wrote *Harry Potter and the Sorcerer's Stone* at a table in a café during her baby's naps.

   2. J. K. Rowling was divorced and living on public assistance in Edinburgh.

I. **1.** The place where open water joins lockfast ice and still waters meet active water currents is called the floe edge.

   2. On tours of the floe edge, visitors can view walruses, bearded seals, beluga and bowhead whales, narwhals, seagulls, pintail ducks, and polar bears.

3. They can also visit ice caves, drink pure glacial water, and encounter hoodoos, strangely contoured sandstone formations carved by wind and weather into 60-foot-high columns.

J. 1. The French impressionist painter Renoir suffered great pain from arthritis.

2. He painted with a brush strapped to his hand.

The Mystery of Tears

Revise the sentences below into a brief explanatory paragraph that speculates on the causes of emotional tears. Use relative clauses whenever possible. Not every sentence will contain a relative clause.

1. Tears are nature's way to keep our eyes wet and cleansed.
2. They are actually drops of saline fluid secreted by a gland.

3. We cry as a reaction to eye irritation.
4. Chopping onions causes irritation.
5. Soap or dust in the eye causes irritation.

6. But why do we shed tears when we are happy?
7. And why do we shed tears when we are sad?
8. Why do we shed tears in pleasure and pain?
9. Why do we shed tears in victory and defeat?

10. Emotional tears have long been a mystery.
11. Such tears are unique to human beings.

12. Some doctors now speculate [this].
13. Through tears our body eliminates certain chemicals.
14. These chemicals build up in response to stress.
15. They create a chemical imbalance in the body.

16. Crying is supposed to make us "feel better."
17. It restores chemical balance to the body.

Making Relative Clauses in Context

Revise the first two sentences of each sequence below into a single sentence with a relative clause. Keep as your main clause the sentence that best relates to the third sentence and leads up to it.

EXAMPLE

Tacos, bagels, and sushi can now be found at fast-food counters every-where. Tacos, bagels, and sushi were once available only in authentic ethnic restaurants. You had to order such food in Mexican cantinas, Jewish delicatessens, or Japanese seafood bars.

Tacos, bagels, and sushi, **which can now be found at fast-food counters everywhere,** were once available only in authentic ethnic restaurants. You had to order such food in Mexican cantinas, Jewish delicatessens, or Japanese seafood bars.

A. Our Puritan ancestors convinced generations of Americans that staying in bed to write and think was a sign of moral and physical decay. Staying in bed to write and think has long been an accepted practice in Europe. In fact, Winston Churchill did much of the strategic planning for World War II propped up in bed with a glass of brandy close at hand.

B. James Dean anticipated the antiestablishment movement of the 1960s. James Dean starred in the 1950s films *East of Eden* and *Rebel Without a Cause.* Dean's portrayal of a defiant teen fighting the status quo was a powerful symbol to the generation of youth who protested the war in Vietnam and racial injustice in America.

C. In Spanish, *querencia* means a place. You know you are safe in the place. Animals feel *querencia* instinctively: salmon spawn in protected rivers, robins build nests out of harm's way, and bears hibernate in sheltered caves.

D. Chewing gum has been commercially popular in the United States for more than 200 years. Chewing gum was made from the resin of spruce bark and paraffin wax but is now manufactured from chicle, the latex or fluid from sapodilla plants. Today, Americans chew 300 sticks of gum annually, on the average.

E. For a healthy snack, sprinkle cumin, curry powder, or Parmesan cheese on popcorn. Your guests will devour the healthy snack. Then set out big bowls of the treat and watch them gobble it down.

As American as Apple Pie

Revise the sentences below to create an explanatory essay that communicates how much American English is a blend of various traditions. Use relative clauses where possible. Not every sentence will contain a relative clause.

1. How American is the American language?

2. It's about as American as jazz.
3. Jazz's Eastern European roots reverberate in the reedy whine of the saxophone.
4. Jazz's African roots reverberate in the rhythmic beat of the drums.

5. It's as American as Levi's.
6. Levi's were developed in the 1848 gold rush by a German immigrant.
7. The German immigrant was named Levi Strauss.

8. Of course, the central core of our language comes from England.

9. But we've borrowed words and phrases from languages as diverse as Hebrew and Tahitian.
10. We've borrowed words and phrases from languages as diverse as Chinese and Navajo.

11. Spanish gave us hundreds of words.
12. They include *barbecue, patio,* and *alligator.*

13. Yiddish gave us *bagel, chutzpah,* and *kosher.*
14. Jews spoke Yiddish in Eastern Europe.
15. African Americans contributed verbal rhythms and rap.
16. As well, African Americans contributed such distinctively American words as *OK* and *Yankee.*

17. We have to thank Native Americans for most of our place names.
18. Our place names are names like Mississippi, Ohio, and Chicago.

19. Every ethnic and national group has left evidence of itself in our language.
20. Every ethnic and national group has blended into the fabric of our country.

21. How American is the American language?

22. It's plenty American. [Make this into a fragment to answer the question above.]

Using Relative Clauses to Control Paragraph Emphasis

Read the following paragraphs in order to decide which sentence in each is out of place. Then strengthen the focus of each paragraph by revising the out-of-place sentence into a relative clause.

EXAMPLE

Dorie Miller won the Navy Cross for shooting down two Japanese planes during the attack on Pearl Harbor. One of the first African American heroes of World War II, Miller was a mess attendant on the USS *West Virginia*. He had never been trained in the operation of a machine gun due to the Navy's racial segregation policies. Nonetheless, his marksmanship was amazing, and his medal cited him for his "distinguished devotion to duty, extreme courage, and disregard for his own personal safety during the attack."

Dorie Miller won the Navy Cross for shooting down two Japanese planes during the attack on Pearl Harbor. One of the first African American heroes of World War II, Miller, **who was a mess attendant on the USS *West Virginia*,** had never been trained in the operation of a machine gun due to the Navy's racial segregation policies. Nonetheless, his marksmanship was amazing, and his medal cited him for his "distinguished devotion to duty, extreme courage, and disregard for his own personal safety during the attack."

A. Jet lag is apparently worse when you travel eastward, against the sun. Your body seems to adjust more easily to a longer day than to a shorter one. The longer day occurs when you travel westward. Morning light coming six hours early on your way to Europe apparently upsets your body's natural rhythm more than the six hours added to a day when you head toward Asia.

B. If your medicine chest doesn't contain an aloe vera plant, it's not well stocked. The aloe vera contains a sap that Native Americans long used as a treatment for minor burns. The aloe vera looks like a cactus. Squeezed on a burn, the sap cools the skin and prevents blisters.

C. According to the book *Psychology and the Internet,* visitors to Internet auction sites can become addicted to bidding on merchandise. These auction sites are open for business twenty-four hours a day. Warning signs of addiction include experiencing a "high" from the activity and a need for increasing amounts of auction participation to achieve that high. Some users need professional care to treat their computer addiction. One Massachusetts hospital recently opened a Computer Addiction Services unit.

Ellis Island: Dream and Nightmare

Revise the sentences below into an explanatory essay about the experiences of immigrants arriving in the United States from Europe in the early 1900s. Use relative clauses where possible. Not every sentence will contain a relative clause.

1. In the Atlantic Ocean, off the shores of New York City and New Jersey, sits Ellis Island.

2. Ellis Island was the first stop in the United States for 16 million European immigrants between 1892 and 1924.

3. The immigrants were a diverse group.

4. These immigrants included craftspeople, farmers, tradespeople, laborers, and intellectuals.

5. Many were political exiles trying to escape persecution.

6. A few were political revolutionaries.

7. They all shared a dream of a new life in a new world.

8. In 1891, the U.S. Bureau of Immigration began to restrict entry to the country.

9. The bureau barred immigrants with mental problems, disease, and criminal records.

10. The immigration officials conducted many rigorous exams.

11. They did this to determine the eligibility of arriving immigrants.

12. They administered a thorough physical.

13. They tested for English literacy.

14. They investigated political beliefs.

15. And they rejected over 4 million applicants.

16. Most of the 4 million were sent back to Europe.

17. However, there was an appeals process.

18. The appeals process required the immigrants to be detained in jail-like dormitories on Ellis Island.

19. The detainees slept in double- or triple-deck beds.

20. The detainees were separated from their spouses.

21. The detainees washed in huge public bathhouses.

22. The public bathhouses could handle 200 people at a time.

23. More than 3,000 rejected detainees committed suicide.

24. They chose to die rather than return to their homelands.

25. Their dreams of a new life had turned into a nightmare.

4

Participles

Preview

This lesson explains how you can construct two kinds of participles—present and past. You make present participles by adding **-ing** to a verb, and you normally make past participles by adding **-ed** or **-d** to a verb, although irregular verbs sometimes have different forms. The lesson will show you how participial phrases can add action and life to sentences as well as suggest relationships instead of stating them explicitly. When you position them properly, participial phrases can create emphasis within a paragraph or even help to hold the paragraph together.

✍ CONSTRUCTING PARTICIPLES

When you first draft a paper, you may have some short, choppy, and repetitive sentences like these from a description of a boxing match:

> The old heavyweight proved an easy knockout victim. He was dazed.
> He was reeling.

As you revise, you can eliminate the repetition and choppiness by changing two of the sentences into participles:

> **Dazed and reeling,** the old heavyweight proved an easy knockout victim.

> OR

> The old heavyweight, **dazed and reeling,** proved an easy knockout victim.

Dazed is a past participle; **reeling** is a present participle.

To construct a present participle, you simply add **-ing** to a base verb form; for example, *read* becomes **reading** and *shake* becomes **shaking.** When you construct a past participle, you generally use the **-d** or **-ed** form of the verb. For instance, *disturb* becomes **disturbed** and *scare* becomes **scared.** For some irregular verbs, the past participle ends in -n or **-en,** so that *throw* becomes **thrown** and *drive* becomes **driven.** For a few other irregular verbs, the past participle has individual forms, so that *sing* becomes **sung,** *go* becomes **gone**, and *stand* becomes **stood.**

❧ PARTICIPIAL PHRASES

A participle often appears with additional words that add details to it. Together, the participle and the additional words form a PARTICIPIAL PHRASE, such as **obviously bored, noisily burping, circled by the hungry sharks,** or **waving vigorously at the TV camera.** Compare the following two sentences:

> The old heavyweight, **dazed and reeling,** proved an easy knockout victim.
>
> The old heavyweight, **dazed by a series of hard punches to his body and reeling from a powerful jab to his head,** proved an easy knockout victim.

A reader might ask of the first sentence, "How had the old heavyweight been dazed?" and "Why was he reeling?" Because it answers those questions, the second sentence is more vivid and descriptive. Participial phrases will help you write prose that satisfies your readers.

❧ USING PARTICIPIAL PHRASES TO CREATE MOVEMENT

Because participles describe so effectively, they can bring your writing to life. Notice how the sentence below becomes more vivid when you add present participial phrases (**-ing** phrases) to the main clause:

> Possums employ a whole range of responses to defend themselves from an enemy.

↓

> Possums employ a whole range of responses to defend themselves from an enemy, **baring their teeth, hissing like an angry cat, clambering up a tall tree, or, as a last resort, falling into a comatose state, body limp and eyes wide open.**

Because they are verb forms, participles add lively, animated action to your sentences. Present participles particularly give this sense of movement. In the next example, you can almost feel the nervousness of the job applicant because the sentence uses the present participles **squirming, rolling, unrolling,** and **reminding:**

The applicant waited alone in the outer office, **squirming on the vinyl chair, rolling and unrolling his résumé, and reminding himself to maintain eye contact during the interview.**

✌ USING PARTICIPIAL PHRASES TO SUGGEST RELATIONSHIPS

You can use participial phrases not only to wake up your sentences with lively movement but also to suggest time– or cause–result relationships. Participial phrases suggest such relationships less directly than clauses beginning with terms like *because, thus, therefore,* and *as a result.* In this way, participles are more subtle. Notice how the introductory clause in the first example below asserts that Anthony Hopkins made Hannibal Lecter frightening because he glared at the camera and did not blink, while the participial phrase in the second example only suggests that by glaring and not blinking, the actor created a frightening screen presence:

> Because actor Anthony Hopkins glared directly at the camera and did not blink for long periods of time, he made the cannibalistic murderer of *Silence of the Lambs,* Hannibal Lecter, a frightening presence on the screen.

↓

> **Glaring directly at the camera and not blinking for long periods of time,** actor Anthony Hopkins made the cannibalistic murderer of *Silence of the Lambs,* Hannibal Lecter, a frightening presence on the screen.

If you revise your early drafts to include structures like participial phrases to suggest relationships, readers will consider your writing sophisticated and interesting. The second example sentence below, because it gives the cause of the vets' problems in the participial phrase **disillusioned by the American public's negative perception of the war,** suggests the result, without having to state it directly, as the first example does in the sentence beginning with *therefore:*

> Some Vietnam vets were disillusioned by the American public's negative perception of the war. Therefore, they suffered severe mental problems when they returned to civilian life.

↓

> **Disillusioned by the American public's negative perception of the war,** some Vietnam vets suffered severe mental problems when they returned to civilian life.

In the following pair, the time relationship that the first example states directly with the word *then*, the second example suggests with a participial phrase:

> We pulled off the interstate. Then we descended the exit ramp to fast-food alley, a long block of deep-fry dens and burger joints stamped out of plastic.

$$\downarrow$$

> We pulled off the interstate, **descending the exit ramp to fast-food alley,** a long block of deep-fry dens and burger joints stamped out of plastic.

Notice also that the participial phrase in the second sentence almost makes it seem as if the car is still moving, since there is no longer a period to stop the motion of the sentence after the word *interstate*.

✌ POSITIONING PARTICIPIAL PHRASES

You can often move participial phrases from one position to another in a sentence—before the main clause, after it, in the middle of it. When you move participial phrases, you change sentence rhythm, shift emphasis, create sentence variety, and even provide links between sentences. Reading your different versions aloud and listening carefully to the variations among them will help you decide just when you can move participial phrases effectively. Consider the following three sentences:

> **Keeping one eye on his professor,** Ricardo quickly scanned the X-Men comic hidden behind his bulky microbiology textbook.
>
> OR
>
> Ricardo, **keeping one eye on his professor,** quickly scanned the X-Men comic hidden behind his bulky microbiology textbook.
>
> OR
>
> Ricardo quickly scanned the X-Men comic hidden behind his bulky microbiology textbook, **keeping one eye on his professor.**

Each version is likely to affect readers differently. In the first, the participial phrase initially captures the readers' attention. It briefly delays the main action of the sentence and perhaps makes readers wonder what will happen, thus heightening the surprise and the humor of the sentence. In the second, the participial phrase interrupts the main action of the sentence, making readers pause twice. These interruptions emphasize *Ricardo* and *quickly,* the words on either side of the commas. The third version places the participial phrase after the main clause, where it becomes a playful commentary on Ricardo's actions.

Sentences with several participial phrases offer you even more choices: you might keep the phrases together or separate them in various ways. Here are just two variations of a sentence with several phrases:

Grandma always arrives in the "Blue Bullet," her '86 Celica, **plunging into our driveway, screeching to a halt, tooting her horn, and grinning ear to ear.**

OR

Tooting her horn, Grandma always arrives in the "Blue Bullet," her '86 Celica, **plunging into our driveway, screeching to a halt, and grinning ear to ear.**

While the first sentence opens with Grandma's arrival, the second sentence makes readers wait a bit; in fact, readers "hear" Grandma tooting the horn on her '86 Celica before they even know that she has arrived. If you put participial phrases in different places, you can emphasize different aspects of Grandma's colorful and memorable behavior.

How can you decide where to position a participial phrase? Sometimes the relationship between the phrase and the main action of the sentence will tell you the right sequence. If the phrase describes something that happened before the main action of the sentence, the phrase—like these two past participial phrases—will precede that main action:

Introduced only thirty years ago, computed tomography (CAT) scans are now available in more than 30,000 locations around the world.

Portrayed by Julia Roberts on film, Erin Brockovich has become a hit on the lecture circuit, giving motivational talks to groups like bookstore managers or real estate agents.

If the phrase describes something that happened after the main action of the sentence, the phrase—like the following present participial phrase—will follow that main action:

Soo Mi opened the brightly wrapped package, **discovering a small wooden box held shut by a silver clasp.**

Sometimes you can use present participial phrases to suggest that two actions are occurring simultaneously, whether the phrases come before or after the main clause:

Carrying the cumbersome bass drum in front of me, I jostled my way through the stubborn crowd to the bandstand.

OR

I jostled my way through the stubborn crowd to the bandstand, **carrying the cumbersome bass drum in front of me.**

Sometimes the relationships between sentences will help you figure out where to place a participial phrase. In the next sentence, the phrase **dealing with current technology rather than ghosts or goblins** may occur before or after its subject:

Dealing with current technology rather than ghosts or goblins, contemporary legends preserve the basic structure of classic horror tales.

OR

Contemporary legends, **dealing with current technology rather than ghosts or goblins,** preserve the basic structure of classic horror tales.

But within the context of the following paragraph, you would more likely place the participial phrase at the beginning of its sentence:

Modern life produces its own folk tales, called urban legends. **Dealing with current technology rather than ghosts or goblins,** contemporary legends preserve the basic structure of classic horror tales. One such tale concerns an elderly woman who accidentally cooks her dog while trying to dry him in her microwave oven.

When it introduces the second sentence, the participial phrase not only separates the two occurrences of the word *legends,* but more important, it also explains the nature of urban legends, connecting the first sentence and the main action of the second. In that way, it helps to hold the paragraph together. Placed correctly, participles and other modifiers form transitions between sentences.

❧ IMPROPERLY ATTACHED PARTICIPLES

You can sometimes make a sentence awkward or even cause confusion when you begin it with a participle. The following example suggests that the crowd, not the quarterback, limped away from the huddle:

The injured quarterback limped away from the huddle.

The sympathetic crowd cheered the injured quarterback.

↓

Limping away from the huddle, the sympathetic crowd cheered the injured quarterback.

The awkwardly placed participle is called a *dangling participle* or *dangling modifier.* The sentence is more clear if you make "the quarterback" the subject of the main clause, thus keeping the participle from dangling:

Limping away from the huddle, the quarterback was cheered by the sympathetic crowd.

Here the participial phrase also suggests a cause–result relationship, since it is the quarterback's heroic action of playing while hurt that triggers the crowd's sympathetic cheers.

✒ PLAYING WITH PARTICIPLES

In the next several pages, you'll have an opportunity to play with participles, creating them, moving them around, revising with them. When you're drafting or revising your own papers, remember to look for opportunities to use participles. They can make your writing more readable, more detailed, and more interesting.

EXERCISES

Constructing Participial Phrases

I. Revise each sequence of sentences below into a single sentence by converting the marked sentences into participial phrases. Move the phrases to different positions until the sentences sound right to you.

EXAMPLE

1. ~~He was~~ slowed by Parkinson's disease.
2. Muhammad Ali moved deliberately among the adoring children at the mall.
3. ~~He~~ signed autographs.
4. ~~He~~ shook hands.
5. And ~~he~~ spoke in a soft voice.

↓

Slowed by Parkinson's disease, Muhammad Ali moved deliberately among the adoring children at the mall, **signing autographs, shaking hands, and speaking in a soft voice.**

OR

Signing autographs, shaking hands, and speaking in a soft voice, Muhammad Ali, **slowed by Parkinson's disease,** moved deliberately among the adoring children at the mall.

A. 1. ~~A team of scientists~~ relied on DNA extracted from a preserved giant dodo.

 2. A team of scientists has concluded that genetically the extinct bird was just an overgrown pigeon.

B. 1. To cook like an Italian, you have to immerse yourself in the production of a meal.

 2. ~~You have to~~ stir the sauce.

 3. ~~You have to~~ add the herbs and spices.

 4. ~~You have to~~ reduce the liquid.

    5. ~~You need to~~ enjoy the warmth and aromas around you.

    6. ~~You need to~~ trust your palate.

    7. And then ~~you need to~~ share what you have prepared with others.

C. **1.** E.T. fools Elliott's mom.

    2. ~~He~~ stands perfectly still in Elliott's closet.

    3. ~~He~~ pretends to be a stuffed toy.

D. **1.** ~~Chicago's Wicker Park neighborhood was~~ settled first by German and Scandinavian immigrants.

    2. Chicago's Wicker Park neighborhood began drawing Polish newcomers in the 1860s.

E. **1.** ~~Polar bears~~ propel themselves with their front legs.

    2. Polar bears can dive up to fifteen feet deep into icy arctic waters.

II. Revise each sequence below into a single sentence by converting one or more of the original sentences into a participial phrase. If the sentences allow, write more than one version for each sequence.

EXAMPLE

    1. Roughly 45,000 thunderstorms ravage the earth every day.

    2. They drench the countryside with torrential rain.

    3. They buffet buildings and trees with howling winds.

Roughly 45,000 thunderstorms ravage the earth every day, **drenching the countryside with torrential rain and buffeting buildings and trees with howling winds.**

OR

Drenching the countryside with torrential rain and buffeting buildings and trees with howling winds, roughly 45,000 thunderstorms ravage the earth every day.

F. **1.** On January 15, 1919, a building exploded at a Boston distillery.

    2. It suffocated 21 workers in a thick, noxious ooze of black molasses.

G. **1.** The locomotive lumbered into Grand Central Station.

    2. It skidded along the tracks.

3. It splashed sparks onto the passenger platform.

4. It discharged gray puffs of steam.

5. It finally screeched to a halt.

H. 1. The Beatles were inspired by Chuck Berry and Buddy Holly.

   2. The Beatles added strings, new percussion, jazz rhythms, and folk melodies.

   3. They expanded the boundaries of '50s rock and roll.

   4. They set the stage for a succession of performers from Jefferson Airplane to Garth Brooks.

I. 1. The tourists stepped through the door of the Chinese tea shop.

   2. The tourists were inundated by the tantalizing smells of roses, lilacs, honeysuckle, and pungent green twigs.

J. 1. The gray whales observed the tour boat from afar.

   2. The gray whales touched the craft with their snouts and refused to leave until the startled tourists petted them.

Eat and Run

Using participial phrases whenever appropriate, revise the following sentences into a lighthearted paragraph that makes a connection between two generations, their dating behavior, and their eating habits. Not every sentence will contain a participle; you'll be able to use other structures as well. Add details of your own similar to those in Sentence 2.

1. How different were the teens of the 1950s from today's teens?

2. Teens of the 1950s may have dressed in unfamiliar poodle skirts and black leather jackets.

3. They had familiar problems.

4. Their problems were these.

5. They didn't know where to go on a date.

6. They didn't have much money to spend on a date.

7. But some teens in Des Plaines, Illinois, found an answer.

8. Their answer solved these teenage dating problems once and for all.

9. Teens lined up to eat at the new Golden Arches "fast-food" restaurant.

10. A museum now stands on this hallowed spot.

11. The museum is called Museum Number 1 Store.

12. The museum commemorates a momentous event in American teen history.

13. In the parking lot, visitors will find cars from the 1950s.

14. Inside the museum, they will find the original menu.

15. The menu featured only 15-cent burgers, 19-cent cheeseburgers, and 10-cent fries.

16. Museum Number 1 Store was devoted to the concept of "fast" food.

17. It provided no seats for its customers.

18. It was so simple.

19. Guys bought their girls a quick bite.

20. After this, they stood and gobbled their McMeal.

21. They zoomed off to their local sock hop or drag race.

22. Burger meals for under a dollar have become extinct.

23. They have gone the way of the poodle skirt and the sock hop.

24. Today's teens still eat and run at the Golden Arches.

25. But now teens have a new problem.

26. They're not sure who pays.

27. Is it the guy?

28. Is it the girl?

Creating Participial Phrases

I. Add details and illustrations to the following sentences by using participial phrases. Add both a past and a present participial phrase to at least two of the sentences.

EXAMPLE

I stared at my mom for a minute.

↓

Horrified at her latest fashion statement, I stared at my mom for a minute, examining the small gold ring in her eyebrow.

A. The door creaked open.

B. The coach screamed at the referee.

C. The United States depends on oil and gas for most of its energy needs.

D. The toddler threw his half-eaten banana at the nearby crowd of shoppers.

E. The horsefly buzzed into the kitchen.

II. Choose one of the five sentences below, or write a sentence of your own. Then, with that sentence as your focus, write a brief paragraph that includes several details in the form of participles.

EXAMPLE

Rachel added her new doctor's appointment to her PDA.

Tapping her stylus rapidly on the display area of her PDA, Rachel added her doctor's appointment to the week's calendar. She attached a note to the appointment, **reminding her to take along her prescription bottles.** Finally, she held down the scroll button, **navigating through her address book and inserting the doctor's phone number right after her dentist's.**

A. Kim rapidly punched the buttons in the elevator.

B. They tentatively reached out their hands toward each other.

C. The pilot managed to pull himself from the wreckage before it burst into flame.

D. Ellen quickened her pace to a trot.

E. The driver buckled his seat belt.

Underground Railroad

When you combine the following sentences, you will have an explanatory essay that reflects on the tragedy of slavery in the pre–Civil War period. Revise the sentences, using as many participial phrases as you can to make your essay clear and forceful. Not every sentence should contain a participial phrase.

1. The Underground Railroad was not a railroad made of steam and steel.

2. But it was a secret network of people determined to help fugitive slaves escape from bondage.

3. Its routes led north from the slave states to Canada.

4. Its routes wound their way through the Midwest and New England.

5. The fugitives crossed hundreds of miles of dangerous territory.

6. The fugitives moved from station to station on foot.

7. They slept in barns and churches.

8. They were assisted by brave and dedicated abolitionists.

9. One abolitionist in Elkhart County, Indiana, sympathized with the fugitives.

10. Elkhart County is located south of Lake Erie.

11. He decided to help fugitives.

12. He made his house into a station on the Underground Railroad.

13. He constructed a fireplace in his basement.

14. He kept the fugitives warm during the cold Lake Erie winter.

15. Subsequent owners of the house have converted it into an inn.

16. But they have kept the basement in good condition.

17. They have kept it as a tribute to the Underground Railroad.

18. Cold travelers still stay in the basement.

19. Cold travelers are warmed by the working fireplace.

20. Today, the inn's guests merely defy the wrath of the icy Lake Erie winter.

21. Yesterday, the Underground Railroad's "guests" defied the wrath of inhuman slave hunters.

Making Participles in Context

Each of the passages below is too wordy and needs a sharper focus. Reduce the wordiness and sharpen the focus by revising at least one of the sentences into a participial phrase.

EXAMPLE

Marbles were just about the most popular game for centuries in Asia, Europe, and both the Americas. It was especially popular in small-town

America, particularly during the Great Depression. Marbles were cheap in those days, costing only a nickel. In recent decades, thousands of members have been attending the Marble Collectors Society of America annual show. The members trade marbles for $75 to $300. The most expensive marble, the gold-banded Lutz, was made in Germany before World War I and is worth over $5,000.

Marbles were just about the most popular game for centuries in Asia, Europe, and both the Americas. It was especially popular in small-town America, particularly during the Great Depression. Marbles were cheap in those days, costing only a nickel. In recent decades, thousands of members have been attending the Marble Collectors Society of America annual show, **trading marbles for $75 to $300**. The most expensive marble, the gold-banded Lutz, was made in Germany before World War I and is worth over $5,000.

A. As we entered the main room of the nursing home, I saw my grandfather sitting bent over in his chair. He rummaged through the bag on his walker. And he pulled out one item then another to place on the table before him. These were his remaining possessions—a few photographs, an alarm clock, a book, and a pocketknife he'd owned since childhood. I had never realized until then just how much his life had diminished from the joyous freedom of childhood to the joyless confinement of old age.

B. Of all the plants on earth, the poppy has perhaps the most far-reaching potential for good and ill. When it is processed legally into codeine and morphine, it provides us with drugs unsurpassed in treating extreme pain. When it is processed illegally into heroin, it brings addiction and misery to hundreds of thousands. It is at once a blessing and a curse.

C. As smoke began to fill the kitchen, the janitor sprinted out of the cafeteria. She coughed painfully and raced for the school's front door. She gasped for air. She strained to hear the fire engines. But all that she could hear were her own rasping efforts to inhale. Would she be able to make it outside, or would she pass out? Her chest tightened, but with a final lunge, she burst through the door and gulped down the cold winter air.

Of Gems, Kings, and Curses

Using participial phrases wherever appropriate, revise the following sentences and combine them into an essay that tells the story of a famous diamond, reputed to be cursed. Not every sentence will contain a participle; you'll be able to use other structures as well. If you can, add details for vividness, and make whatever other changes you feel will improve the essay.

1. The Hope Diamond is a combination of not only gray but blue.

2. The blue is caused by boron in the stone.

3. The Hope Diamond is oval shaped.

4. The Hope Diamond weighs over 45 carats.

5. The Hope Diamond has a mysterious cursed history.

6. The diamond was mined in India in the 1600s.

7. It was purchased as a 112-carat rough-cut diamond by a French jewel trader.

8. The jewel trader sold it to King Louis XIV of France.

9. King Louis had it cut into a 67-carat triangle diamond.

10. The diamond was soon called the "French Blue."

11. The French Blue passed from King Louis XIV to his son, Louis XV, and then to his grandson, Louis XVI, over the next 120 years.

12. During the French Revolution, Louis XVI lost his head.

13. And during the French Revolution, the French Blue disappeared.

14. Six decades later, Henry Philip Hope, a British gem collector, flaunted a large 45-carat blue diamond.

15. His display earned the former French Blue a new name: the Hope Diamond.

16. But what about the infamous curse?

17. In the twentieth century, a wealthy American family purchased the stone.

18. The family suffered many tragedies including one divorce, one nervous breakdown, and four deaths.

19. Then the family donated the Hope Diamond to the Smithsonian Institution in 1958.

20. It is on display in Washington, DC.

21. Was the family's donation merely a generous bequest to a famous museum?

22. Was the family's donation a prudent effort to escape a lingering curse?

23. No one can be sure.

24. After all, one of its royal owners not only lost the diamond.

25. King Louis also lost his head.

5

Appositives

Preview

This lesson explains how to revise by using appositives. You construct appositives by deleting a subject noun and "to be" verb from a sentence, leaving a noun phrase or an adjective phrase that defines or summarizes a noun phrase it sits next to. When you punctuate an appositive, you typically use commas, dashes, or colons.

✌ USING APPOSITIVES

Sometimes when you're writing, the information you put in one sentence identifies or defines something you've said in another:

> Farmers try to control the poinsettia whitefly by digging up entire fields of infested crops. The poinsettia whitefly is a pesticide-resistant superbug.

Pairs of sentences like this sound choppy and repetitious. You can avoid such choppiness and repetition in several ways. You might make one sentence into a relative clause as you learned in the third lesson:

> Farmers try to control the poinsettia whitefly, **which is a pesticide-resistant superbug,** by digging up entire fields of infested crops.

But you can often express information that defines and identifies information like "a pesticide-resistant superbug" in even fewer words as an AP-POSITIVE:

> Farmers try to control the poinsettia whitefly, **a pesticide-resistant superbug,** by digging up entire fields of infested crops.

APPOSITIVE means being positioned next to something. Generally, you position an appositive next to the noun that it identifies, whether that noun is at the beginning or the end of a sentence:

> Deborah Tannen's *You Just Don't Understand,* **a book about the problems of communication between men and women,** suggests that the two genders see the world in different ways.

Attending college in America made Hideki homesick for his family, his friends, and even the roadside *jinja*—**the small shrines that dot the land of Japan.**

❧ CONSTRUCTING APPOSITIVES

You can construct an appositive by revising any sentence in which a noun phrase follows the verb **to be (is, are, was, were).** Eliminate the subject and the verb, insert commas or dashes, and you have an appositive. By eliminating the subject, **peanut butter,** and the verb, **is,** from the second sentence below, you can change the remaining noun phrase, "the favorite food of American children," into an appositive:

In 1904, a St. Louis doctor introduced peanut butter as a health food for the elderly. ~~Peanut butter is~~ the favorite food of American children.

↓

In 1904, a St. Louis doctor introduced peanut butter—**the favorite food of American children**—as a health food for the elderly.

❧ USING APPOSITIVES TO DEFINE, SUMMARIZE, AND EXPLAIN

Appositives help you sharpen the focus of a passage because they expand the meaning of nouns; they supply defining or identifying details about them, as in the poinsettia whitefly example above. Here are some further illustrations. In the first, the appositive **an ancient Chinese calculating machine** defines "an abacus." In the second, the appositive **a thirteenth-century Scottish nobleman** identifies "William Wallace":

Many Asian merchants still add by moving beads on an abacus, **an ancient Chinese calculating machine.**

In *Braveheart,* Mel Gibson played William Wallace, **a thirteenth-century Scottish nobleman.**

Appositives not only give defining details but also explain ideas more fully. The appositive in the next example expands the idea about the fact that "major airlines are merging with regional carriers and cutting flights," by calling it **a trend that intensified after 9/11:**

To avoid bankruptcy, some major airlines are merging with regional carriers and cutting flights, **a trend that intensified after 9/11.**

With short summarizing appositives—appositives of one or two words—you can produce a striking effect, especially at the end of a sentence, where they bring a reader to a jarring halt and emphasize your point:

> Half an hour later, the second police diver returned with the same report—
> **nothing.**

Longer summarizing appositives can fill in important background information. Here is a long appositive that sets the current economic status of the American South and West into historical perspective:

> The Sun Belt states of the South and West—**states that remained rural
> and backward during the industrialization of our country**—have come to
> dominate the U.S. economy during the technological revolution.

Sometimes you can drive a point home with a summarizing appositive punctuated as a fragment. Here's one that humorously emphasizes the topic of a whole paragraph, the size of an elephant bird's egg:

> Clomping about the island of Madagascar, elephant birds, extinct for
> hundreds of years, laid eggs that rivaled in size any egg ever known.
> Intact fossil specimens are occasionally found over a foot across. These
> masterpieces of motherhood could have held the goods from 7 ostrich
> eggs, 180 chicken eggs, or 12,000 hummingbird eggs. **Some omelet!**

When you pack appositives into a series, they summarize by listing characteristics:

> Midwesterners will long remember the sudden devastation of the Flood
> of '97: **the destroyed homes, the waterlogged storefronts, the impass-
> able streets, the underwater ghost towns.**

> In Aesop's fables, the animals that overcome great odds represent qual-
> ities we want for ourselves: **power, intelligence, thoughtfulness, and
> honesty.**

✷ USING APPOSITIVES TO SHOW NEGATIVE QUALITIES

Sometimes the best way to explain something is by saying what it is not. You can do just that with negative appositives:

> Less than fifty feet past the intersection, the old VW Beetle started mak-
> ing unusual noises, **not its familiar rattles and knocks.**

> Bloodhounds are gentle creatures, **not the vicious beasts their name
> would suggest.**

You can also make a generalization with a negative appositive:

The movie *The Shipping News* is structured in fragments, punctuated by disarming humor, and peopled with quirky, likable characters— **not the typical Hollywood love story.**

✌ USING ADJECTIVES AS APPOSITIVES

Whether positive or negative, appositives are normally nouns. But other structures can sometimes function as appositives. You can make adjectives into appositives if you move them from their normal position in front of the noun they modify. Here is a sentence with adjectives (**honest, fun-loving, affectionate, wonderful**) in their usual position before a noun:

My blind date turned out to be an honest, fun-loving, affectionate, and wonderful person.

Now here are three of these adjectives—**honest, fun-loving,** and **affectionate**—shifted to the end of the sentence to function as appositives:

My blind date turned out to be a wonderful person—**honest, fun-loving, and affectionate.**

If you read the two versions out loud, you'll notice that the one with the list of appositive adjectives more clearly focuses on the fact that "my blind date turned out to be a wonderful person." Appositive adjectives summarize qualities and can help you sharpen the focus of sentences. Like appositive nouns, they can be placed at the beginning, middle, or end of a sentence:

Stark, forbidding, awesome, spectacular—Death Valley is a hauntingly beautiful place to visit, despite its name.

Horror novelist Anne Rice's black Harley-Davidson motorcycle— **beautiful, seductive, and hungry**—glides through the streets of New Orleans like a vampire on the prowl.

Shanghai is different from other Chinese cities—**more European, more cosmopolitan.**

✌ USING APPOSITIVES TO FOCUS AND TO LINK SENTENCES

If you have a choice about which of two sentences to reduce to an appositive, you can usually let focus be your guide. What you keep as a complete sentence will generally be your main focus. For instance, you can make either of the next two sentences into an appositive:

Avignon is a walled city in southern France. Avignon was the home of the pope in the fourteenth century.

Let's suppose that the next sentence in your paragraph reads, "It is perhaps the most spectacular of the medieval walled cities in that region." The context suggests that you want your reader to learn more about southern France and about walled cities; you can keep the focus on those topics by making the second full sentence into an appositive and leaving the first as a full sentence:

Avignon—**the home of the pope in the fourteenth century**—is a walled city in southern France. It is perhaps the most spectacular of the medieval walled cities in that region.

If, on the other hand, the next sentence in your paragraph reads, "In fact, the century was a time of confusion in the church, when one pope was housed in Avignon and another was housed in Rome," then the context suggests that you want to inform your readers about the history of the papacy. In that case, you can keep the focus on that topic by making the original first sentence into an appositive, leaving the second as a full sentence:

Avignon—**a walled city in southern France**—was the home of the pope in the fourteenth century. In fact, the century was a time of confusion in the church, when one pope was housed in Avignon and another was housed in Rome.

Although the most common position for an appositive is immediately *after* the noun that it defines, an appositive can also be placed at the beginning of a sentence. Such an opening appositive can be an especially effective link between sentences. Notice how the appositive **a man who never baked a cake in his life** serves as a bridge between the next two sentences:

High on the list of America's most successful food industrialists stands Duncan Hines. **A man who never baked a cake in his life**, Hines founded a multimillion-dollar food products company that names its line of premium cake mixes after him.

ॐ USING SPECIAL APPOSITIVES

Certain appositive structures have special forms. Some appositives call for the repetition of the noun, others for an appropriate pronoun, and still others for a connective to link them to a main clause.

Whenever several words separate an appositive from the noun it defines, try repeating the noun. In the next sentence, the word *magazines* in the appositive repeats *magazines* in the main clause:

> Millions of Americans now read magazines that did not even exist a mere decade ago—**magazines that focus on the Internet, extreme sports, and CD-ROM computer games.**

With a list, you can repeat the noun several times or simply include it once:

> Oprah showed heartwarming stories unfolding in every corner of the nation—**stories of neighbor helping neighbor, stories of cops befriending gang members, stories of teens "adopting" grandparents.**

> OR

> Oprah showed heartwarming stories unfolding in every corner of the nation—**stories of neighbor helping neighbor, cops befriending gang members, teens "adopting" grandparents.**

Repeating a noun works well, especially when the appositive includes a long modifier:

> Satirist Al Yankovic (known as "Weird Al") writes and performs many song and music video parodies—**parodies like "Eat It," "My Bologna," "Amish Paradise," and "Running with Scissors."**

But sometimes you may prefer to introduce the appositive with a pronoun like **one, that, the latter, something,** or **the kind,** rather than repeat the noun:

> Satirist Al Yankovic (known as "Weird Al") writes and performs many song and music video parodies—**ones like "Eat It," "My Bologna," "Amish Paradise," and "Running with Scissors."**

When your appositive provides an example or illustration, you can relate it to the main clause with a connective like **namely, including, especially, particularly, notably, mainly,** or **for example:**

> A number of U.S. presidents—**including Lincoln, Roosevelt, and Kennedy**—have died in office.

> For the first time on network TV, sitcoms **in the '90s, notably *Ellen, Roseanne, Spin City*, and *Will and Grace*,** introduced gay and Lesbian characters and situations into their story lines.

Sometimes you can even use an appositive to explain another appositive. Notice how in the next example the appositives **home owners** and **not skilled gardeners** explain the first appositive **people like themselves.**

> Liz and Jeff Ball wrote *Yardening* for people who just happen to take care of grass and plants, **people like themselves, home owners, not skilled gardeners.**

✄ PUNCTUATING APPOSITIVES

Appositives are generally set off by commas, dashes, or colons. The different punctuation marks create different effects. Notice how in the first version below, the comma, because it is such a common form of punctuation, hardly calls attention to itself or to the appositive phrase, **an intellectually nurturing environment.** In the second example, the dash—because it creates a longer pause—makes the appositive more emphatic. The colon makes the third version seem more formal:

> The decades-long rise in I.Q. scores nationwide may be explained by one fact, **an intellectually nurturing environment**.

> The decades-long rise in I.Q. scores nationwide may be explained by one fact—**an intellectually nurturing environment**.

> The decades-long rise in I.Q. scores nationwide may be explained by one fact: **an intellectually nurturing environment**.

When you have a series of appositives separated by commas, it's usually best to set the series off by a dash or colon. In the next example, the single appositive, **an offbeat biologist,** is set off by a comma; the series of appositives—**face mites, body lice, and tooth amoebas**—are separated by commas and set off by two dashes:

> The squiggly creatures that live on people—**face mites, body lice, and tooth amoebas**—are the subject of a book by Roger Knutson, an offbeat biologist.

✄ PLAYING WITH APPOSITIVES

The following exercises give you opportunities to construct and use appositives in various contexts, in order to explain, define, or summarize nouns. Take the opportunities the exercises provide to learn how to use appositives effectively. You'll learn best if you play with the exercise sentences, experimenting with alternate versions and moving them to different sentence positions.

Remember to use appositives in your own writing. Why not try them in the next paper you write?

EXERCISES

Constructing Appositives

I. Revise each sequence below into a single sentence by converting the marked sentences into appositives. Punctuate the appositives with commas, dashes, or colons, as you see fit.

EXAMPLE

  1. In Rwanda, Dian Fossey lived among and studied gorillas.

  2. Gorillas are shy, beguiling animals whose numbers have been decimated by poachers.

In Rwanda, Dian Fossey lived among and studied gorillas—**shy, beguiling animals whose numbers have been decimated by poachers.**

  A. **1.** In recent years several computer-generated movies have revolutionized film animation.

      2. ~~One was~~ *Toy Story.*

      3. ~~One was~~ *Shrek.*

      4. ~~One was~~ *Ice Age.*

  B. **1.** Mark Mathabane tells in *Kaffir Boy* of his involvement in the 1976 Soweto Township protests.

      2. ~~Mark Mathabane~~ is a native of South Africa.

      3. ~~The Soweto Township protests were~~ street demonstrations in which hundreds of black South Africans were killed by the police.

  C. **1.** The huge waves caused by earthquakes are known as *tsunami.*

      2. ~~They are~~ not *tidal waves* as many people think.

  D. **1.** The cartoon *Dilbert* exposes the essential defining features of the corporate working environment.

      2. ~~The essential defining features of the corporate working environment are~~ hypocrisy, inefficiency, contradiction, and excess.

E. **1.** Harry Potter excels at Quidditch.

2. ~~Quidditch is~~ a magical hybrid of soccer and basketball played on flying broomsticks.

II. Revise each sequence below into a single sentence by converting one or more of the original sentences into an appositive. If the sentences allow, write more than one version for each sequence. Punctuate the appositives with commas, dashes, or colons, as you see fit.

EXAMPLE

1. A typical Swiss army knife includes a variety of tools.

2. The tools include a watch.

3. The tools include a tiny pen.

4. The tools include a nail file.

5. The tools include a screwdriver.

6. The tools include a metal saw.

7. The tools include pliers.

8. And the tools even include a fish scaler.

A typical Swiss army knife includes a variety of tools, **tools like a watch and tiny pen, a nail file and screwdriver, a metal saw and pliers, and even a fish scaler.**

OR

A typical Swiss army knife includes a variety of tools: **a watch, a tiny pen, a nail file, a screwdriver, a metal saw, pliers, and a fish scaler.**

F. **1.** Human immunodeficiency virus (HIV) breaks down the body's immune system, leaving the infected person defenseless against infections that a healthy body can easily fight.

2. ~~HIV is~~ the virus that causes AIDS.

G. **1.** Beatles fans by the thousands trek to Liverpool each year for a magical mystery tour of Fab Four shrines.

2. ~~One Fab Four shrine is~~ Strawberry Fields.

3. ~~One Fab Four shrine is~~ Abbey Road.

4. ~~One Fab Four shrine is~~ the grave of Eleanor Rigby.

5. And ~~other Fab Four shrines are~~ the boyhood homes of John, Paul, George, and Ringo.

H. 1. The first ready-made clothes were scorned by the American public when they appeared in the early 1800s.
   2. ~~The first ready-made clothes were~~ crude.
   3. ~~The first ready-made clothes were~~ cheap.
   4. ~~The first ready-made clothes were~~ shapeless.

I. 1. A debate has erupted in the scientific community about the ethics of cloning.
   2. ~~Cloning is~~ the replication of DNA.
   3. ~~DNA is~~ the genetic material that all living organisms are made of.

J. 1. Though paleontologists once described them as huge, lumbering creatures, scientists now believe dinosaurs were surprisingly active animals.
   2. ~~They believe dinosaurs were~~ energetic.
   3. ~~They believe dinosaurs were~~ agile.
   4. ~~They believe dinosaurs were~~ fast on their feet.

Having a Whale of a Time

Revise the sentences below by combining them into a description of whale watching, a growing summer tourist activity. Not every sentence should contain an appositive; you'll be able to make other structures as well as appositives.

1. From April to October, whaling boats depart from New England and eastern Canadian harbors.
2. The whaling boats often sail to Stellwagen Bank off Provincetown, Massachusetts.
3. Stellwagen Bank is a good spot to find whales.

4. These boats are filled with tourists who want to go whale watching.
5. These boats are not filled with hunters who want to kill whales.

6. Whale watching has become an increasingly popular pastime.
7. Whale watching is a pastime that attracted 3.6 million whale watchers in the United States in 1994.

8. When you join in and take up whale watching, you need to know what to look for to spot a whale.

9. You can look for a very small, far-off undramatic puff of water and air from the whale's spout.

10. And you can look for the puff to appear again fifteen seconds later.

11. You can also look for dark specks in the sky above the water.

12. The dark specks in the sky are gannets, herring gulls, and terns that dive on the same fish schools that attract whales.

13. From the whale-watching boats, spectators sometimes see a glistening black back of a fin whale.

14. They can also spot the dorsal fin of a humpback whale.

15. Sometimes they can gaze down the throat of a North Atlantic right whale when it opens its mouth.

16. The reaction to a whale sighting is always the same.

17. The reaction to a whale sighting is always a chorus of "oohs" and "aahs" and a round of cheers.

Creating Appositives

I. Revise each of the following sentences by adding at least one fact or detail in the form of an appositive. For one sentence, add a series of appositives.

EXAMPLE

Some 2,000 companies have produced cars in the United States.

Some 2,000 companies have produced cars in the United States—**a number that is no longer likely to grow.**

OR

Some 2,000 companies have produced cars in the United States, **companies such as Hudson, Nash, Packard, Studebaker, and, of course, General Motors.**

OR

Some 2,000 companies—**U.S. and foreign**—have produced cars in the United States.

   A. College life is a series of shocks.

   B. Sean rushed outside with his new double-barreled water gun.

   C. Kylie remembered how thoughts of the dark cellar had filled her with numb excitement.

   D. These are the characteristics of an effective teacher.

   E. Teenagers often wear clothes their parents dislike.

II. Select one of the five sentences below, or write a sentence of your own. Then, with that sentence as your focus, write a brief paragraph that includes several details in the form of appositives.

EXAMPLE

My grandmother hated to exercise.

My grandmother hated to exercise. She used to mock Mom for working out every morning to Heather Locklear tapes. Then Gram injured her back in a car accident—**a rear-end crash on I-40**. She was in a body cast for about three months. On the advice of her physical therapist, she began exercising, doing knee bends and sit-ups, slowly at first, just for a few minutes at a time. After about six months, Gram graduated to aerobics, **the final step in the hospital's rehabilitation program**. She loved it. She dances and stretches to the music with the best of them. Now she's more limber than Mom, **almost as good as Heather Locklear.**

   A. The old rocking chair reminded Sofia of her grandfather.

   B. The speaker's self-assurance and humor set the tone for the graduation ceremony.

   C. Siblings often have similar interests and talents.

   D. My cousin Vinnie took vitamins by the handful.

   E. *Hamlet* ends in a bloody melee.

Beam Me Up, Cookie Monster

Revise the sentences below to create an explanatory essay about what the Nabisco symbol on Oreos really means. Not every sentence will contain an appositive; you'll be able to make appositives as well as other structures. Read your revision aloud, and try to hear it as your readers will, as a means of deciding how to combine these sentences.

1. Have you ever noticed the circle-and-cross design on Oreos?
2. Oreos are the world's favorite cookies.

3. Perhaps you should pay attention the next time you peel the chocolate cookie apart.
4. You pull it apart to get to the white stuff in the middle.

5. People who look for secret messages in company logos claim [this].
6. The design is an intergalactic transmission code.

7. Nabisco representatives say [this].
8. The design is actually a Renaissance printer's mark.
9. The company borrowed it for a logo in 1898.
10. It is not an intergalactic signal.

11. Earth kids think Oreos are out of this world.
12. The cookie company never meant to communicate with extraterrestrials. [Make one of these two sentences into a clause beginning with **though**.]

13. Is it any wonder?
14. E.T. preferred Reese's Pieces.

Appositives in Context

Each of the passages below has several sentences that would be more effective as appositives. Reduce the wordiness and sharpen the focus of the passages by revising those sentences into appositives and placing them appropriately.

EXAMPLE

Archaeologists are discovering that family life and relationships may not have changed much since biblical times. As they dig into the ancient cities of the Middle East, scientists find remnants of everyday life. These remnants would have crumbled away long before now in damper climates. One recent archaeological expedition found 2,000-year-old papyrus letters written by a youth away from home. The dig was in Egypt. Roughly translated, the letters read, "Dear Mom and Dad, Please send money."

Archaeologists are discovering that family life and relationships may not have changed much since biblical times. As they dig into the ancient cities of the Middle East, scientists find remnants of everyday life—**remnants that would have crumbled away long before now in damper climates**. One recent archaeological expedition, **a dig in Egypt,** found 2,000-year-old papyrus letters written by a youth away from home. Roughly translated, the letters read, "Dear Mom and Dad, Please send money."

A. Costume designer Judianna Makovsky thought that J. K. Rowling's illustrations of Quidditch uniforms weren't elegant enough. Quidditch uniforms were rugby shirts and red capes. So she costumed the film actors in eclectic athletic gear. The gear was preppie sweaters and ties, nineteenth-century fencing breeches and arm guards under their wizard robes.

B. Editors of a leading business magazine set out to write a story about the corporate world's ten toughest bosses. But when they did, they immediately ran into a problem. The problem was fear. Subordinates who managed to overcome their apprehensions enough to grant secret interviews helped the editors to pinpoint one key quality of the "tough ten" right away. It was the bosses' ability to inspire respect tinged with terror.

C. Why are babies twice as likely to be born at midnight as at noon? Why do rejection rates for organ transplant patients jump sharply on the seventh, fourteenth, twenty-first, and twenty-eighth day after surgery? According to chronobiologists, the reason is that our internal organs move through mysterious but predictable cycles. Chronobiologists are scientists who study the rhythmic motions in plant and animal life. These cycles last minutes, days, months, and even years.

A Small Act

Revise the sentences below to create an explanatory essay about Rosa Parks's act of defiance. Not every sentence will contain an appositive; you'll be able to make appositives as well as other structures. Read your revision aloud, and try to hear it as your readers will, as a means of deciding how to combine these sentences.

1. History is often changed by small acts.

2. Small acts are like that of Rosa Parks.

3. Rosa Parks boarded a bus for home after work.

4. She was a seamstress in a department store.

5. This was on December 1, 1955.

6. This was in Montgomery, Alabama.

7. She was tired.

8. And her feet ached.

9. She took a seat in the first row of the "Colored Section."

10. The law demanded this.

11. The bus filled.

12. At that time the driver ordered her to give up her seat to a white man.

13. Rosa refused.

14. She remained seated.

15. And she was arrested.

16. That evening, civil rights leaders asked African Americans not to ride on Montgomery's buses.

17. The leaders included young Martin Luther King, Jr.

18. Rosa Parks sparked one of the major victories in the civil rights movement.

19. This was the famous Montgomery Bus Boycott.

20. The boycott led to the desegregation of institutions throughout the United States.

21. She destroyed segregation [in this way].

22. It was by her small but defiant act.

LESSON 6

Absolutes

Preview

In this lesson, we look at absolutes, phrases that look like sentences but lack the verb **be,** and allow you to add details to sentences, just as other modifiers do. You construct absolutes by deleting **be** or by changing a verb into its **-ing** form. Absolutes can help you suggest cause–effect and before–after relationships in a sentence and are the only modifying phrases that allow you to focus on specific parts of a scene. Using absolutes can suggest that you are a skillful and adroit writer.

❧ ABSOLUTES

Suppose in a paper describing your friend as she studies late one night, you begin by writing two sentences:

> Maria was sitting at her desk. Her head was slightly lowered over a pile of chemistry notes.

When you revise, you may decide you want your reader to see the close connection between Maria's sitting at her desk and her head lowered over her work, so you join the two sentences with an *and:*

> Maria was sitting at her desk, and her head was slightly lowered over a pile of chemistry notes.

But you're still not happy with this version. So you give it another try, and you write the following sentence:

> Maria was sitting at her desk, **her head slightly lowered over a pile of chemistry notes**.

This version is concise and links the details of Maria's sitting at her desk to her head lowered over her notes. What you've done is to turn the original second sentence into an ABSOLUTE—a phrase that is almost but not quite a complete sentence and which you can use to show the parts of a scene sketched out in the main clause.

77

✑ CONSTRUCTING ABSOLUTES

There are two ways to construct absolutes from full sentences. One way is to remove a form of the verb *be*—such as *is, are, was,* or *were.* If you remove the word *was* from the sentence

Her head was slightly lowered over a pile of chemistry notes.

you can create the absolute

her head slightly lowered over a pile of chemistry notes

A second way to construct an absolute is by changing the main verb into its **-ing** form. In the following sentences about an ominous evening, for example, you can change the verbs *gusted* and *gave* into *gusting* and *giving* in order to produce a pair of absolutes:

The evening grew ominous. The breeze gusted more strongly. Whitecaps gave the lake a frothy, sinister appearance.

The evening grew ominous, **the breeze gusting more strongly, and whitecaps giving the lake a frothy, sinister appearance.**

You can construct absolutes using either of these two methods—removing the verb *be* or changing a verb to its **-ing** form. The method you choose will depend on the sentences you are trying to revise.

✑ ADDING DETAILS

Like other modifiers—relative clauses, participles, and appositives—absolutes can make your writing more forceful and more sophisticated. They also help you to add details to your writing, giving it greater texture. Absolutes have one special characteristic: because they have their own subjects, absolutes allow you to shift from a description of a whole to a description of its parts. Remember how the earlier example began by describing Maria and then concluded by focusing on her lowered head? That's exactly how absolutes shift from a larger scene to a part. In the next example, the absolute shifts the reader's attention from the birch tree as a whole to its branches:

The sickly birch tree struggled to grow.

The sickly birch tree struggled to grow, **its scrawny branches stretching up through shadows toward the sunlight.**

In the same way, the two absolutes in the next example add details about the John Cleese scene; these details help readers see the humor of the comic's situation because they focus on the small details—the parrot and the parrot's feet—turning an otherwise normal scene, a man leaving a pet store, into a hilarious one:

> My favorite John Cleese routine shows the British comic leaving a pet store.

$$\downarrow$$

> My favorite John Cleese routine shows the British comic leaving a pet store, **a dead parrot on his shoulder, its feet nailed to its perch.**

More than any other modifier, absolutes break larger scenes into their component parts.

✎ INDICATING CAUSE AND EFFECT

Not only can absolutes add vivid details to your sentences by allowing you to move from whole scenes to parts of scenes, but they can also suggest cause–result relationships. Suppose, for example, that you wanted to revise the sentences below in order to indicate that the sinking of the battleship was caused by the torpedoes that tore apart its stern:

> The stern of the battleship was torn apart by torpedoes. The battleship slowly sank into the Pacific.

Your first impulse may be to write:

> Because its stern was torn apart by torpedoes, the battleship slowly sank into the Pacific.

This sentence is perfectly acceptable, but you can suggest the same cause–result relationship more concisely and more subtly with an absolute:

> **Its stern torn apart by torpedoes,** the battleship slowly sank into the Pacific.

Though you can generally move absolutes to several positions in a sentence, when you use an absolute to suggest a cause–result relationship, it's best to place it at the beginning, as in the battleship sentence above.

✎ POSITIONING ABSOLUTES

Cause–result or time relationships will often determine whether an absolute will work at the beginning, middle, or end of a sentence. An absolute that refers to an earlier event normally appears before the main clause. Notice that sometimes absolutes which begin sentences sound better when they are introduced by the preposition *with:*

> Their emperor was killed in an ambush. The 30,000-strong Incan army retreated before Pizarro's 180 conquistadors.

↓

> **Their emperor killed in an ambush,** the 30,000-strong Incan army retreated before Pizarro's 180 conquistadors.

OR

> **With their emperor killed in an ambush**, the 30,000-strong Incan army retreated before Pizarro's 180 conquistadors.

An absolute that refers to an event occurring later than the event in the main clause should generally follow the clause:

> Gene Kelly began "Singin' in the Rain" softly, **his voice rising to an exuberant crescendo before fading back to echo the familiar opening bars.**

But when an absolute does not suggest cause or a time relationship, you can position it almost anywhere in the sentence, at the beginning, the end, or even in the middle of the sentence:

> **Their faces lined with exhaustion,** the firefighters trudged back to their truck.

OR

> The firefighters trudged back to their truck, **their faces lined with exhaustion.**

OR

> The firefighters, **their faces lined with exhaustion,** trudged back to their truck.

Sometimes you will want to move an absolute from one sentence position to another for the sake of variety or rhythm. The next example sounds better if you move the absolutes next to the subject, separating the subject from the predicate:

> Alicia Keyes looked elegant at the Grammy ceremony—**her eyes shimmering with glittery eye shadow, her hair pulled back in a formal style.**

> Alicia Keyes—**her eyes shimmering with glittery eye shadow, her hair pulled back in a formal style**—looked elegant at the Grammy ceremony.

Other things being equal, though, absolutes work best at the ends of sentences. And that's where writers most often put them:

> Dorothy hesitantly took her first steps down the Yellow Brick Road, **Toto clutched in her arms.**

> Richard Nixon looked uncomfortable when he walked, **shoulders hunched, arms hanging at his sides.**

Unless they relate to time– or cause–result, you can move absolutes to different sentence positions.

❧ ABSOLUTES IN A SERIES

Like other modifiers, absolutes may be used in a series. A series of absolutes can be particularly forceful when you want to build the ideas in a sentence toward a climax:

> The new pilot brought the crippled airplane safely down for an emergency landing, **her heartbeat finally slowing, her clenched hands gradually releasing the controls, her relief visible.**

The absolute **her relief visible** has to be the final item in the series because the sentence would not make sense if it appeared elsewhere. To hear the difference, try reading the sentence aloud with **her relief visible** as either the first or second item. Placed at the end, **her relief visible** explains what it means when the pilot's heartbeat slows and her clenched hands release the controls, an explanation that just doesn't make sense if it appears before the other absolutes.

Knowing that a series of absolutes gains power when its items are placed in order of increasing importance, how would you combine these sentences?

> After the prom, the gymnasium was in chaos. A torn banner dangled from the ceiling. The once-beautiful decorations were simply a mess. Burst balloons were scattered all over the floor.

Since the sentence *The once-beautiful decorations were simply a mess* essentially summarizes the chaos in the gym, you should probably place it at the end of the series when you make the clauses into absolutes:

> After the prom, the gymnasium was in chaos, **a torn banner dangling from the ceiling, burst balloons scattered all over the floor, the once-beautiful decorations simply a mess.**

If a series of absolutes builds to a climax, start with the specific details and move to the more general ones.

✿ USING ABSOLUTES WITH OTHER STRUCTURES

Absolutes are especially useful because they fit together with other structures to give your sentences variety and texture. Notice how you can improve the next four sentences by combining them into a single sentence that includes an appositive and a past participial phrase and ends with an absolute:

> Chagall's *Bella au Col Blanc* is a sensitive portrait of the artist's first wife. Her name was Bella. She is dressed in a low-cut dark dress. A wide, white collar sets off her graceful features and black hair.

> Chagall's *Bella au Col Blanc* is a sensitive portrait of the artist's first wife, Bella, dressed in a low-cut dark dress, **her graceful features and black hair set off by a wide, white collar.**

Because such combinations of structures are compact and rhythmically interesting, they provide you with useful stylistic options.

✿ PUNCTUATING ABSOLUTES

You generally separate an absolute from other sentence parts with a comma:

> Elephants hear through their feet, **the soft skin of the foot acting like a drumhead to sense vibrations.**

But if you want to emphasize the details in the absolute, you may use a dash:

> Elephants hear through their feet—**the soft skin of the foot acting like a drumhead to sense vibrations.**

A dash can be especially effective when you have to separate a series of modifiers from a main clause. Here is a sentence with a long, involved series of absolutes. The dash separates the series from the main clause, while the commas separate the individual absolutes:

> Several Apache helicopters circled overhead—**their machine guns flashing yellow, enemy soldiers returning the fire, the battlefield a confusion of bullets, screams, and explosions.**

Notice how the dash helps to emphasize the series by making the reader pause just a bit longer before reaching the vivid descriptive details that follow.

✏ USING ABSOLUTES TO TIGHTEN PARAGRAPHS

It's easy to miss opportunities to create absolutes. But if you pay careful attention to your writing, you can often find opportunities to change a sentence into an absolute, helping you to tighten up paragraphs and making your writing appear more sophisticated. Here's an example of a nicely written paragraph about plant communications that is made even better by changing one sentence into an absolute. Read both paragraphs out loud to hear how the small change makes the second paragraph sound more "together," its ideas more tightly bound, more compact.

> You don't hear the chemical "noises," but your plants may be holding conversations with each other. Botanists have discovered that plants can send out cries for help, invitations, even warnings. Each is in the form of odor molecules. For instance, plants send chemical cues to repel insect enemies and signals that invite other insects that eat the insects eating the plant. What's more, nearby plants can listen to this conversation and set up their own defenses.

> You don't hear the chemical "noises," but your plants may be holding conversations with each other. Botanists have discovered that plants can send out cries for help, invitations, even warnings, **each in the form of odor molecules.** For instance, plants send chemical cues to repel insect enemies and signals that invite other insects that eat the insects eating the plant. What's more, nearby plants can listen to this conversation and set up their own defenses.

✏ PLAYING WITH ABSOLUTES

In the next few pages, you'll have an opportunity to play with absolutes, constructing them and moving them around in sentences, learning how to place them effectively and deciding how to punctuate them effectively with commas and dashes. When you're drafting or revising your own papers, remember to look for opportunities to use absolutes. They can make your writing more economical, powerful, and subtle.

EXERCISES

Constructing Absolutes

I. Revise each group of sentences below into a single sentence by converting the marked sentences into absolutes. Move the absolutes to different positions until the sentences sound right to you.

EXAMPLE

The huge combine cut its way steadily through the winter wheat. Its blade ~~was~~ churning.

↓

Its blade churning, the huge combine cut its way steadily through the winter wheat.

OR

The huge combine—**its blade churning**—cut its way steadily through the winter wheat.

OR

The huge combine cut its way steadily through the winter wheat, **its blade churning.**

A. **1.** The dragon kite soared across the afternoon sky.

　　2. Its long green tail whipped in the wind

B. **1.** Two young women stood together on the subway platform.

　　2. One ~~was~~ in knee socks and bundled pigtails.

　　3. ~~She was~~ folding and unfolding a street map.

　　4. The other ~~was~~ in a plaid skirt and peasant blouse.

C. **1.** It was a perfect morning for a hike.

　　2. The air ~~was~~ crisp.

　　3. The sky ~~was~~ steel blue.

　　4. Fleecy clouds ~~were~~ studding the sky.

D. **1.** When Mom drives, our Dalmatian sits on her lap.

2. One paw ~~is~~ on the steering wheel.

3. His head ~~is~~ out the window

E. **1.** Houdini was locked in the casket.

2. His arms ~~were~~ confined in a straitjacket.

3. His legs ~~were~~ manacled with chains.

II. Revise each sequence below into a single sentence by converting one or more of the original sentences into an absolute. You can revise some of the sentences into other structures as well.

EXAMPLE

When I walked in, Grandpa was sitting at the kitchen table.

The newspaper was spread before him.

His morning coffee steamed in his mug.

When I walked in, Grandpa was sitting at the kitchen table, **the newspaper spread** before him, his morning **coffee steaming in his mug.**

A. **1.** The maneuvers of the U.S. Air Force Thunderbirds are an awesome sight.

2. The F-16s zoom toward one another at a wicked speed.

B. **1.** I dozed through tenth-grade grammar as the soon-to-retire teacher [construct two absolutes using Sentences 2 and 3] diagrammed sentence after sentence day after day.

2. His nose was red.

3. Gray hair was flowing out of his ears.

4. He was boring me to tears.

C. **1.** Hummingbirds seem to defy the laws of gravity.

2. Their tiny bodies hover in one spot like miniature helicopters.

D. **1.** At the closing bell, the signs of the market crash were everywhere on Wall Street.

2. One trader in stock-index options sobbed, "It's the end of the world!"

E. **1.** High school graduation is a strange ritual.

    2. Boys wear earstuds.

    3. Girls balance on platform shoes.

    4. Parents are ready to set them loose on the world.

Rhyme and Reason

Revise the following sentences into a paragraph on the fun and meaning of Dr. Seuss. Not every sentence will contain an absolute; you'll be able to make other structures as well. Feel free to add details to make your essay more vivid and personal. Don't forget to play with the sentences. Try different versions for different effects.

1. The Dr. Seuss books are great to read aloud.

2. Their quirky characters and clever rhymes please children and adults alike.

3. Everybody loves to read [about this].

4. In some way the Cat in the Hat can destroy a house.

5. He can do this when Mom's gone.

6. And one fish two fish is fun to rhyme with red fish blue fish.

7. But Dr. Seuss often has a serious message.

8. The message accompanies the rhymes and the funny-looking characters.

9. His simple rhyming language tells us to have faith in ourselves.

10. It does this in *Oh, the Places You'll Go.*

11. And who doesn't learn from Sam I Am?

12. We should try new things.

13. After all, you might like green eggs and ham.

14. You can try it even without being on a boat with a fox or a goat.

15. My favorite character is Horton the elephant.

16. He's faithful 100%.

17. He sits on bird eggs through the fall.

18. He sits on bird eggs through the icy cold of winter.

19. And he sits on bird eggs into the spring.

20. He is unlike the good-for-nothing mother bird, Maisie.

21. He understands.

22. He must hatch the eggs.

23. These scenes [construct two absolutes using Sentences 24 and 25] amuse us.

24. An elephant is hatching eggs.

25. A creature is learning to like green eggs with ham.

26. But Seuss teaches us lots of important lessons for life as well.

27. Those lessons include flexibility, self-reliance, and responsibility.

Creating Absolutes

I. To each of the following five sentences add at least one fact or detail in the form of an absolute. Add a series of absolutes to any two of the sentences. Try to make the sentences vivid and lively.

EXAMPLE

Diane stood motionless at the end of the diving board.

Diane stood motionless at the end of the diving board, **tears streaming down her cheeks.**

OR

Diane stood motionless at the end of the diving board, **hands at her sides, heels slightly raised, every muscle anticipating action.**

A. Zach brought home Sheffield, his new golden retriever, from the pet shop.

B. The party turned out to be a lot of fun.

C. A growing percentage of undergraduates hold full-time jobs.

D. The election turned into a landslide.

E. I walked into the pouring rain.

II. Choose one of the next five sentences, or create a sentence of your own, and write a paragraph with it as the controlling idea. Add illustrations and details in the form of absolutes and other modifiers.

EXAMPLE

Her dad had never seen Jenny so happy.

Her dad had never seen Jenny so happy. Her jeans, smeared with mud, were torn at the knees. Her sweatshirt, which had been so bright and yellow that morning, looked like a filthy brown rag. Her untied wet sneakers barely clung to her feet, **their soggy laces dragging on the ground.** Her hair was wild, sticking together in sweaty clumps. But a smile creased her dirt-stained face. "I found a big puddle, Daddy," she exclaimed.

A. It was just the kind of book I wanted to read.

B. From across the street, the house looked deserted.

C. My computer began to act up.

D. Here I am, writing to you.

E. High school students' lives have become more stressful than ever.

Amusement Parks

Revise the following sentences into an essay that suggests how amusement parks appeal to kids of all ages. Not every sentence will contain an absolute; you'll be able to make other structures as well. Feel free to add details in order to make your essay more vivid

1. Amusement parks aren't just for kids anymore.

2. Today's amusement parks are resort areas.

3. They are complete with hotels and nightclubs.

4. They are complete with restaurants and variety shows.

5. Children enjoy the rides.

6. Their cries of delight echo across the park.

7. Parents and grandparents tour flower gardens or watch from shaded benches.

8. Young adults also enjoy the rides.

9. You can see them on the water rides.

10. Their clothes are drenched.

11. Their faces are flushed with laughter.

12. Their arms are linked in friendship.

13. Amusement parks can even be places of romance.

14. Couples walk arm in arm among the flowers.

15. Couples use the rides as an excuse.

16. They cling to one another in public.

17. The couples have their picture taken together.

18. They pose in outrageous costumes.

19. They have their half-eaten candied apples in hand.

20. Their sunglasses are casually shoved up into their hair.

21. The amusement park is a fun place.

22. It is for kids of all ages.

Making Absolutes in Context

Reduce the wordiness and tighten the connections in each passage below by converting at least one of the sentences into an absolute. Revise in other ways as well to improve each passage.

EXAMPLE

Situated on an island in San Francisco Bay, Alcatraz was the most notorious prison in U.S. history. For three decades, Alcatraz housed America's most famous criminals. Its cell blocks were filled with legendary convicts such as Al Capone, Machine Gun Kelly, and Robert Stroud, the "Birdman of Alcatraz." "The Rock," as Alcatraz was called by the prisoners, had the reputation of being escape-proof. And there were but fourteen escape attempts in twenty-nine years. San Francisco Bay's frigid waters and treacherous currents scared would-be escapees. San Francisco Bay discouraged all but the most desperate escape artists. Just one prisoner ever reached the mainland, only to be captured immediately and returned to his cell. Closed as a prison since 1963, Alcatraz remains an ominous and foreboding landmark off the California coast.

Situated on an island in San Francisco Bay, Alcatraz was the most notorious prison in U.S. history. For three decades, Alcatraz housed America's most famous criminals, **its cell blocks filled with legendary convicts such as Al Capone, Machine Gun Kelly, and Robert Stroud, the "Birdman of Alcatraz."** "The Rock," as Alcatraz was called by the prisoners, had the reputation of being escape-proof. And there were but fourteen escape attempts in twenty-nine years. **Its frigid waters and**

treacherous currents scaring would-be escapees, San Francisco Bay discouraged all but the most desperate escape artists. Just one prisoner ever reached the mainland, only to be captured immediately and returned to his cell. Closed as a prison since 1963, Alcatraz remains an ominous and foreboding landmark off the California coast.

A. The two boys leaned against the willow tree beside the stream. Their fishing poles were resting on sticks. Their eyes were gazing at the bobbers floating on the ripples. The fish didn't take the lines but periodically teased the boys, nibbling at the bait and jumping within arm's reach of the bank. The boys tried changing bait and rods and places. Nothing worked. One tiny bluegill did strike late in the afternoon but fell off just as it was drawn near the bank. Because their stomachs were crying for food, because their backs were burning from too much sun, and because their legs were stiff from sitting, both boys gathered their gear and headed for home.

B. Part of a comic strip's appeal is its exploitation of human relationships. Since the early 1900s, comic strips have made fun of some of the most complex of human emotions. Their characters have envy, jealousy, and greed. In one of the first comic strips, Krazy Kat skidded across the page. His feline eyes were filled with adoration for Ignatz Mouse. Ignatz, however, spent his days throwing bricks at Krazy. Today Garfield the Cat bedevils his friend Odie. But deep down we know that Garfield really loves the simple-minded dog. The characters in comic strips have changed, but the Sunday "funnies" still reflect our attitudes about one another and help us laugh at ourselves.

C. If you are experiencing too much stress and looking for a fun way to relieve it, try juggling. Once a skill mastered only by circus performers, juggling is now taught in stress management workshops for doctors, nurses, managers, and others in need of stress relief. With some practice, you might find yourself stepping up close to the wall and juggling some balls on the rebound. Your hands will be drumming the air, and your mind will be freed from the thought of your declining grade point average or your crucial exam tomorrow. Or if you are a fitness enthusiast, for the ultimate in recreation, try "joggling"—juggling balls or beanbags while running around the track.

Remembering the Bomb

Revise the following sentences into an essay that indicates how the Hibakusha remember the atomic bombing of their city. Not every sentence will contain an absolute; you'll be able to make other structures as well.

1. When you see modern Hiroshima, its port is bustling with activity.
2. Its skyline is filled with tall office buildings.
3. It's hard to imagine the destruction that happened there in August 1945.
4. But the Hibakusha remember.
5. The Hibakusha are the survivors of the world's first atomic bombing.
6. Shima Sinada is one of the survivors.
7. She held her four-year-old daughter, Akiko, in her arms.
8. At the same time, she walked down the street less than one mile from ground zero.
9. This was at the moment of the blast.
10. Moments later, Shima rose from the rubble.
11. Her hands were clasped in prayer for her daughter.
12. But Akiko was one of the 80,000 victims of the bomb that day.
13. So now Shima walks down the streets of modern Hiroshima.
14. Its port is bustling with activity.
15. Its skyline is filled with tall office buildings.
16. And she remembers the blinding flash.
17. She remembers the mushroom cloud.
18. And she remembers her daughter, Akiko, dead in the rubble.

Prepositional Phrases and Infinitive Phrases

Preview

This lesson explains how prepositional phrases and infinitive phrases convey details and guide readers through a written text. Because they express such adverbial relationships as place, time, manner, and reason, prepositional phrases give readers the background information and context necessary to understand the other ideas in sentences. Infinitive phrases can help suggest intention or purpose. By moving prepositional phrases and infinitive phrases from one sentence position to another and using them to replace long clauses, you can make writing more concise, more varied, and more interesting.

✌ CONSTRUCTING PREPOSITIONAL PHRASES

You probably can't speak or write more than a few sentences without using a PREPOSITION. By using prepositions, you make relationships more specific among sentence parts, and you establish points of reference for readers, like road signs on a highway. When you tell **about** your job **at** the Taco Bell **near** the mall **outside of** town, argue **for** or **against** prayer **in** public school, brag that your new computer can play chess **like** a master, or explain how engineers turn saltwater **into** fuel **by** a new chemical process—you're using prepositions.

The most common prepositions are **at, by, for, from, like, of, on, to,** and **with;** others include **after, before, between, despite, during, over, through, under, until**, and **without.** Some prepositions consist of more than one word, such as **according to, as far back as, because of, contrary to, except for, in addition to, in compliance with, in the absence of, rather than, such as,** and **thanks to.**

A preposition never occurs by itself. As its name suggests, it is a *pre-position*: it is positioned before a noun or noun phrase, which serves as its object. A preposition together with its object forms a PREPOSITIONAL PHRASE, such as **with us, under the broiling desert sun, because of her previous success in political campaigns,** and **according to the National Weather Service forecast.**

✌ THE ROLE OF PREPOSITIONAL PHRASES

Because prepositional phrases occur so frequently, it's easy to forget how much they can help you write clear, expressive prose. Prepositional phrases clarify statements by indicating how and why actions occur, and they provide the context for statements by indicating when and where actions occur. Notice that the prepositional phrases in the next sentence indicate place:

> I crossed the U.S. 36 bridge and drove **past Elwood, Kansas, across the Missouri's rich farmland, through bustling Troy,** and **up wooded valleys to the West's high rolling plains.**

But the prepositional phrases do more than indicate place. They encourage readers to feel the movement **past, across, through,** and **up,** until—along with the writer—we get **to** the West's high rolling plains.

In the next example, the prepositional phrase **after the *Challenger* disaster** indicates time; it tells when Americans began to realize the dangers of space exploration:

> **After the *Challenger* disaster,** Americans realized that space exploration had tremendous risks.

Besides place and time, prepositional phrases can also indicate such adverbial concepts as manner, reason, likeness, and condition, as in the following sentences:

> *Manner:* **With a flick of her wrist**, the pizza chef spun the fresh dough high into the air.
>
> *Reason:* **Because of his ability to speak Spanish,** Art received several teaching offers from Texas elementary schools.
>
> *Likeness:* **Like Swiss army knives,** some Stone Age tools served multiple purposes—scraping, cutting, and drilling.
>
> *Condition:* Vegetarians get plenty of protein from nuts and dairy products, whole grains, and beans, **despite the common belief that only meat provides adequate amounts of protein.**

❧ REDUCING CLAUSES TO PREPOSITIONAL PHRASES

Sometimes you can substitute a prepositional phrase for an entire clause to make your writing more concise. You may also find that when a full clause doesn't quite convey the precise relationship you intended between two ideas, you can use a prepositional phrase to clarify your ideas. In the next example, the clause **although they have a menacing appearance** becomes the prepositional phrase **despite their menacing appearance:**

~~Although they have a~~ menacing appearance, most reptiles aren't really vicious if you leave them alone.

Despite their menacing appearance, most reptiles aren't really vicious if you leave them alone.

As you revise your early drafts, you might look closely to see where you can reduce clauses to more concise prepositional phrases.

❧ BALANCED PHRASES

You can use prepositions to create balanced phrases, either in pairs or by repetition in a series. When you use paired prepositions such as **from . . . to, with . . . without, before . . . after,** or **for . . . against,** you imply that you've balanced opposites or even suggest that you've completely covered a subject:

Louis Armstrong performed with musicians of every stripe. He performed with blues singer Bessie Smith, and with classical conductor Leonard Bernstein.

Louis Armstrong performed with musicians of every stripe, **from** blues singer Bessie Smith **to** classical conductor Leonard Bernstein.

A series, on the other hand, lists parallel points and links them in a rhythmic chain that strengthens their relationship:

The Chinese have built a society **with** an educational system radically different from ours, **with** aspirations challenging some of our most cherished values, and **with** a sense of mission both enviable and frightening.

Just as they can heighten relationships between phrases within a sentence, paired prepositions can heighten relationships between sentences in a paragraph. From the two sentences below, it's clear that the Pony Express made mail delivery from one coast to another much faster:

> Mail t California from Massachusetts took up to six long weeks by ship. But then the Pony Express was started, and the same mail took only ten days.

But when you open the first sentence with **before,** you make the reader anticipate a second sentence that begins with **after:**

> **Before** the Pony Express, mail to California from Massachusetts took up to six long weeks by ship. **After** the Pony Express, the same mail took only ten days.

In fact, linking sentences with either a pair or a series of prepositions is one way you can achieve coherence and emphasis between sentences. Notice that by repeating the preposition **under** in the next pair of sentences, you not only link the sentences tightly but also emphasize how much worse things became in Eastern Europe under communism:

> While the czar ruled, only the single nation of Russia was oppressed. But during the rule of the Communist Party, many Eastern European nations, such as Lithuania and Estonia, were also enslaved.

↓

> **Under** the czar's rule, only the single nation of Russia was oppressed. **Under** the Communist Party's rule, many Eastern European nations, such as Lithuania and Estonia, were also enslaved.

Prepositional phrases are simple, easy to use, and functional. They can help you orient your readers and clarify your sentences.

❧ CONSTRUCTING INFINITIVE PHRASES

Similar in appearance to prepositional phrases are phrases made with AD-VERBIAL INFINITIVES. Such infinitive phrases are always introduced by the word **to** or the phrase **in order to** followed by either a simple verb form (as in **to see, in order to write,** or **to daydream**) or a verb phrase (as in **to earn money for college** or **in order to recycle newspapers**). Adverbial infinitives generally imply something that a person might want to do:

> My friends and I hoped our bikes could sound like a motorcycle. My friends and I would clip a baseball card onto the spokes with a clothespin which would make that sound.

↓

To create the sound of a motorcycle on our bikes, my friends and I would clip a baseball card onto the spokes with a clothespin.

✍ POSITIONING INFINITIVE PHRASES

While the sentence about the bicycles has the infinitive at the beginning, you may also use adverbial infinitive phrases at the end of a sentence:

Medical students serve an internship **in order to gain firsthand experience in treating patients.**

The desperate accountant embezzled thousands from her company **to pay her gambling debts.**

When you use an infinitive phrase in the middle of a sentence, it creates an interesting rhythmic variation by separating the subject from its predicate. In the next example, the infinitive phrase interrupts the sentence, creating just a bit of suspense for readers who may wonder what the EPA researchers have done:

EPA researchers, **in order to measure the damage done to forests by air pollution,** are exposing trees to auto emissions, then spraying them with "homemade" acid rain.

You can use either commas or dashes to separate infinitive phrases from main clauses. Because dashes create longer pauses than commas, they give added emphasis to the phrases, especially in the middle or at the end of a sentence:

The desperate accountant embezzled thousands from her company—**to pay her gambling debts.**

EPA researchers—**in order to measure the damage done to forests by air pollution**—are exposing trees to auto emissions, then spraying them with "homemade" acid rain.

Infinitive phrases, like prepositional phrases and other modifiers, can occur in a series, either before or after a main clause:

To commemorate Rosa Parks's courage, to honor her resolve, and to inspire young people, Troy State University-Montgomery erected the Rosa Parks Library and Museum.

For variation, you may omit the word **to** after the first infinitive in a series:

To commemorate Rosa Parks's courage, honor her resolve, and inspire young people, Troy State University-Montgomery erected the Rosa Parks Library and Museum.

Phrase-length modifiers with adverbial infinitives can often replace whole clauses:

> Because she wants to erase the traditional image of God as a man, our minister refers to God as a woman.

> **To erase the traditional image of God as a man,** our minister refers to God as a woman.

❧ MISUSED INFINITIVE PHRASES

Sometimes you have to be careful when you use infinitive phrases, especially when you begin a sentence with one. Readers will expect that an infinitive phrase at the beginning of a sentence is going to say something about the subject of the main clause that immediately follows it. In the following example, readers will anticipate that the person showing delight over the cheese will be the next person mentioned in the main clause:

> **To show his delight with his first taste of Camembert cheese,** Napoleon kissed the waitress who served it to him.

But notice what happens if the main clause begins with the waitress rather than Napoleon:

> **To show his delight with his first taste of Camembert cheese,** the waitress who served it to him was kissed by Napoleon.

In this sentence, readers will be confused about who was delighted—the waitress or Napoleon. Be careful when you place infinitives in sentences so that you do not confuse your readers.

❧ PLAYING WITH PREPOSITIONAL PHRASES AND INFINITIVE PHRASES

In the remaining pages of this lesson, you'll have opportunities to try out prepositional phrases and infinitive phrases, constructing them, moving them around, using them to strengthen relationships among ideas. As you revise or draft your own writing, be sure to look for opportunities to apply what you've practiced in using prepositional and infinitive phrases; they can help you write more concisely and with a stronger sense of focus.

EXERCISES

Constructing Prepositional Phrases
and Infinitive Phrases

Revise each set of sentences below into a single sentence using one or more prepositional phrases (Example I) or infinitive phrases (Example II).

EXAMPLE I: PREPOSITIONAL PHRASES

1. There are a greater number of women in the workforce.
2. Women still earn less than men. [Combine these sentences by starting the first sentence with the preposition **in spite of** or **despite**.]

In spite of a greater number of women in the workforce, women still earn less than men.

OR

Despite a greater number of women in the workforce, women still earn less than men.

A. 1. There are short movie stars like Dustin Hoffman, Michael J. Fox, and Danny DeVito.
   2. The myth that movie heroes have to be tall has been dispelled. [Combine these sentences by starting the first sentence with the preposition **thanks to** or **because of.**]

B. 1. There has been overwhelming evidence since the 1960s that smoking causes cancer and emphysema.
   2. Tobacco companies did not admit the relationship between smoking and illness until 1997. [Combine these sentences by starting the first sentence with the preposition **in spite of** or **despite**.]

C. 1. The U.S. entertainment industry produces the second-largest trade surplus of any American industry.
   2. The reason is the extensive export of motion pictures and of music and videocassette recordings. [Combine these sentences by starting the second sentence with the preposition **because of** or **thanks to.**]

D. 1. There were layers of dirt and dust.

   2. The rolltop turned out to be a handcrafted colonial antique. [Combine these sentences by starting the first sentence with the preposition **beneath** or **under.**]

E. 1. They are racing in the Special Olympics.

   2. Wheelchair athletes also raced in the Atlanta and Barcelona Olympic Games. [Combine these sentences by starting the first sentence with the preposition **beyond** or **in addition to.**]

EXAMPLE II: INFINITIVE PHRASES

1. The waterskier wanted to begin her run.

2. So she yelled, "Hit it!" to her boyfriend driving the motorboat.

The waterskier, **in order to begin her run,** yelled, "Hit it!" to her boyfriend in the motorboat.

OR

In order to begin her run, the waterskier yelled, "Hit it!" to her boyfriend in the motorboat.

F. 1. The auditorium management wanted to prevent crowd-control problems.

   2. The auditorium management initiated reserved seating for rock concerts.

G. 1. The aim of the school was helping students understand death as the natural end of a life cycle.

   2. The school introduced a noncredit course entitled "Death."

H. 1. Cactus is a surprising plant.

   2. Cactus can be used to make jellies and preserves.

   3. Cactus can be used to produce medicines.

   4. Cactus can even be used to build furniture.

I. 1. In 1929, William Dreyer added walnuts and marshmallow bits to chocolate ice cream.

   2. He wanted to make a new ice-cream flavor—Rocky Road.

J. 1. They wanted to prevent adultery.

   2. Early Puritans employed such deterrents as whipping, branding, and imprisonment.

Diana, Princess of Hearts

Using prepositional phrases and infinitive phrases whenever appropriate, revise the following sentences into a draft that describes Princess Diana's life. Not every sentence will contain a prepositional phrase or an infinitive phrase; you'll be able to make other structures as well. As you write this exercise, feel free to add details from your own experience that might make it more informative.

   1. The English have embraced queens.

   2. Their embrace is from Elizabeth I in the sixteenth century to Elizabeth II in the twentieth.

   3. But the English have never embraced a princess in the way they embraced Diana, Princess of Wales.

   4. She married Prince Charles in 1981.

   5. At that time she was an awkward teenager.

   6. She was a fairy-tale princess with a cloud of hair dripping over her eyes.

   7. The press thought [this].

   8. She would grow into a beautiful queen.

   9. She became a symbol of beauty and glamour and chic motherhood.

   10. This happened between 1981 and 1997.

   11. The royal family wanted her to act like a British royal.

   12. They wanted her to act prim and proper, a bit stodgy.

   13. Instead, she remained a lively, down-to-earth young woman.

   14. She was likely to be photographed in jeans, taking her sons to McDonald's.

   15. She was likely to be photographed in an evening gown attending the opera with the rich and famous. [Combine the last two sentences with a "just as . . . as."]

   16. Diana threw herself publicly into helping the victims of illness and war.

   17. This happened after her divorce from Charles.

18. She died in a tragic auto accident.

19. She was fleeing from the photographers.

20. The photographers constantly intruded into her private life.

21. This happened in death as in life.

22. Diana straddled the world where fairy tales come true and the world where children die of AIDS.

23. She never became queen.

24. But she became the Princess of Hearts.

25. This happened for millions around the world.

Reducing Clauses

I. Make each of the following sentences more concise by reducing one or more of the full clauses to a prepositional phrase according to the instructions. Rearrange other parts of the sentences when necessary.

EXAMPLE

There is a lot of damage ultraviolet rays can do to tattoos, and as a result many people are growing more careful than ever about getting too much sun. [Reduce the opening clause to a prepositional phrase beginning with the preposition **because of.**]

Because of the damage ultraviolet rays can do to tattoos, many people are growing more careful than ever about getting too much sun.

A. An Elvis record collection is incomplete if it doesn't include a copy of "Viva Las Vegas." [Reduce the *if* clause to a prepositional phrase beginning with the preposition **without.**]

B. When you see sunlight passing through a glass prism, sunlight shows up as a spectrum of colors: red, orange, yellow, green, blue, indigo, and, finally, violet. [Reduce the opening clause to a prepositional phrase beginning with the preposition **after.**]

C. The Bermuda Triangle mystery has not been reinforced by eyewitness reports, but similar mysteries, like UFOs, Bigfoot, the Loch Ness Monster, and the Abominable Snowman, have been reinforced by eyewitness reports. [Reduce the opening clause to a prepositional phrase beginning with the preposition **unlike**.]

D. Bat wings have a skin covering over the top and bottom of their bones, and they have blood vessels and nerves in between. [Reduce the second independent clause to a prepositional phrase beginning with the preposition **with**.]

E. Cookie historians know that Fig Newtons were named after the Massachusetts town of Newton, near the Kennedy Biscuit Works, although there is widespread belief that they were named for Sir Isaac Newton. [Reduce the clause beginning with *although* to a prepositional phrase beginning with the preposition **despite**.]

II. Make each of the following sentences more concise by reducing one or more of the full clauses to an infinitive phrase. Rearrange parts of the sentence when necessary.

EXAMPLE

The Nigerian writer Chinua Achebe wrote his powerful novel *Things Fall Apart* because he wanted to educate his people about their own history.

The Nigerian writer Chinua Achebe wrote his powerful novel *Things Fall Apart* **in order to educate** his people about their own history.

F. If they wish to make their bread dough rise properly, bakers must dissolve yeast in water that is just the right temperature: 105–115° F.

G. If you hope to make the best possible first impression, your résumé should be free of all spelling and typographical errors.

H. My cousin took up skydiving because he hoped to overcome his fear of heights.

I. If you want to leave a message, record your number after the "Beep!"

J. Officer Suarez, who wanted to hit the bull's-eye consistently, steadied her revolver with both hands.

Inca Express

Using prepositional phrases and infinitive phrases wherever appropriate, revise the following sentences into an essay that explains how an ancient people solved the problem of long-distance communication. Not every sentence will contain a prepositional phrase or an infinitive phrase; you'll be able to make other structures as well.

1. The Incas wanted to rule their vast empire effectively.

2. For this reason, the Incas needed an efficient system of long-distance communication.

3. They lacked both telegraphs and horses.

4. They had to develop a highly organized express message system.

5. They used messengers called *chasquis*.

6. The first *chasqui* would memorize a message for the Lord Inca.

7. He would carry a conch shell, a mace, and a slingshot in his sack.

8. The messenger would start the long journey to Cuzco, the Inca capital. [Combine these sentences by making a prepositional phrase that begins with the preposition **with**.]

9. The messenger carried the weapons for a reason.

10. The reason was to protect himself from enemies.

11. He would blow on the conch shell as he neared the next *chasqui* station.

12. The next *chasqui* station was one and one-half miles away.

13. A fresh messenger would be waiting at the station.

14. A fresh messenger would memorize the message.

15. Then a fresh messenger would carry it to the next station.

16. The message would travel from one station.

17. The message would travel to the next station.

18. The message would eventually reach the Lord Inca.

19. The *chasqui* messenger service could cover 1,250 miles in five days.

20. The *chasqui* messenger service could average more than ten miles per hour.

21. It was a true Inca express.

Using Prepositional Phrases and Infinitive Phrases in Context

The paragraphs below lack focus and coherence because some sentences are wordy and others are not clearly related to one another. Strengthen each paragraph by using prepositional phrases and infinitive phrases to revise those weak sentences. Make whatever other changes you think might strengthen the paragraph. Be sure to write out the complete paragraph.

EXAMPLE

Bach's life differed little from the lives of other musicians in the eighteenth century unless you consider the fact that he wrote better musical compositions. When he was alive, Bach was an obscure musician, trudging from court to court for jobs as choirmaster or organist. He remained obscure for more than 100 years. But his music was "discovered" in the nineteenth century. Our own century considers Bach's work impervious to time and the composer himself a living presence to whom almost everyone in music is somehow indebted. We consider the Beatles indebted to him, and Beethoven was indebted to him as well.

↓

Except for the quality of his musical compositions, Bach's life differed little from the lives of other musicians in the eighteenth century. **During his lifetime,** Bach was an obscure court musician, trudging from court to court for jobs as choirmaster or organist. He remained obscure for more than 100 years, until his music was "discovered" in the nineteenth century. Music lovers of our own century consider Bach's work impervious to time and the composer himself a living presence to whom almost everyone in music, **from Beethoven to the Beatles,** is somehow indebted.

A. There are obvious differences in size and appearance between elephants and humans. Elephants and humans still share similar characteristics. Elephants live to the same age as humans, at times reaching the age of seventy. You can compare them to humans also in that elephants can live almost anywhere, whether in dry savannas or dense rain forests. When they need to change their environment, they use their strength to tear down trees, thus creating grasslands. Elephants are also among the most intelligent of mammals, and they have been known to recognize human friends a decade after their last encounter. They have one fatal weakness—their ivory tusks can be made into beautiful human jewelry.

B. Choosing a hat to wear isn't always as simple as it sounds. In Turkey, the fez, which is made from red felt, was popular as long ago as the eleventh century. But early in the twentieth century, Turkey's rulers wanted to westernize their nation. Turkey's rulers abolished fezzes as part of that country's national dress. Tradition-conscious Turks who insisted on wearing the fez changed their minds. They changed their minds because government executions of several fez wearers took place. Sometimes the simple choice of a hat, it seems, has had deadly consequences.

C. The earliest known depiction of juggling is Egyptian, dating back to 1900 B.C. A terra cotta statue from ancient Thebes, circa 200 B.C., shows a juggler with balls balanced on different parts of his body. There are many such illustrations of juggling. Written references to juggling are also quite old. One Chinese book from 500 B.C. describes a man who could keep seven swords in the air. According to the Hebrew Talmud, Rabbi ben Gamaliel could catch and throw eight flaming torches; Rabbi ben Gamaliel did not drop any of the torches. And the Irish hero Cuchulain juggled nine apples, according to Irish written sources from the fifth century A.D. These ancient jugglers most commonly used knives, torches, and balls. If you wanted to break the current world records for most objects juggled at one time, you would have to juggle more than eight clubs, eleven balls, or twelve rings.

A Fair to Remember

Using prepositional phrases and infinitive phrases whenever appropriate, make the following sentences into an essay that explains why the Chicago World's Fair of 1893 is still remembered today. Not every sentence will contain a prepositional or an infinitive phrase; you'll be able to make other structures as well.

1. The Chicago World's Fair in 1893 may have been the greatest World's Fair in history.

2. The Chicago World's Fair cost more than $27 million to construct.

3. The Chicago World's Fair attracted over 27 million visitors.

4. The Fair included many exhibits from faraway countries.

5. The exhibits included an Algerian theater, a Brazilian concert hall, an East Indian bazaar, a Japanese village, an Egyptian street, and a Viennese

café. [Combine these two sentences by reducing the second sentence to a balanced phrase using **from . . . to.**]

6. The Fair showed visitors famous sights from around the world.
7. The Fair featured a miniature Eiffel Tower, a panorama of Mt. Kilauea, a Hawaiian volcano, and a model of Blarney Castle.
8. Blarney Castle had a replica of the Blarney Stone for tourists to kiss.

9. The Fair's organizers wanted to show visitors how people lived and worked all over the world.
10. The Fair's organizers created exhibit halls where artisans demonstrated their skills.

11. The exhibit halls included a functioning glassworks.
12. In the glassworks, glassblowers provided free souvenirs.

13. In the International Dress and Costume Pavilion, native women from more than forty nations modeled expensive gowns.

14. More than just educational activities were included.
15. Fair-goers could have fun riding a balloon to a height of 1,500 feet or attending Hagenback's Menagerie, an animal show and circus. [Combine these two sentences by reducing the first sentence to a prepositional phrase that begins with **in addition to.**]

16. But the World's Fair may be best remembered for its technological and commercial innovations.
17. The world's first elevated electric railway was exhibited.
18. Thomas Edison's kinetograph was demonstrated.
19. The kinetograph was a forerunner of the movie projector. [Combine the last three sentences by using a prepositional phrase that begins with **such as.**]
20. The Fair had a moving sidewalk.
21. The sidewalk transported passengers at six miles per hour.

22. The Ferris Wheel carried passengers 250 feet up for two revolutions.
23. The Ferris Wheel was invented for the World's Fair.

24. Many visitors wanted to bring home mementos of their visit to the Chicago World's Fair.

25. Many visitors purchased the U.S. Mint's first commemorative coins or the U.S. Post Office's first picture postcards.

26. Hungry visitors could get their fill of many brand-new food products.

27. Many brand-new food products were introduced at the Fair.

28. The new food products included Cracker Jack, Cream of Wheat cereal, Juicy Fruit gum, Pabst beer, Aunt Jemima syrup, diet soda, shredded wheat cereal, and hamburgers.

29. The Chicago World's Fair was a fair to remember.

30. The Chicago World's Fair left a legacy that still influences our lives more than a century later.

8

Coordination and Subordination

Preview

When you coordinate structures, you imply that they are weighted equally. You can put them together with simple coordinators, paired coordinators, or series coordinators. Another way to put structures together is to use subordination. Subordinating one clause to another usually indicates that the material you've placed in the subordinate clause is not as important as the material placed in the main clause. When you use subordination to make two sentences into one, you can begin to shape entire paragraphs as well as strengthen your sentence structure.

❧ SIMPLE COORDINATION

In everyday talking and writing, we use coordination more than any other composing strategy. It's so simple and so basic that all of us were coordinating almost as soon as we began to talk. We often put together words, phrases, and clauses into simple coordination patterns:

> Students ~~like the new history textbook because it tells interesting stories.~~
> Teachers like the new history textbook because it tells interesting stories.

$$\downarrow$$

> **Students and teachers** like the new history textbook because it tells interesting stories.

> Sarah Hughes was happy with her performance in the Olympics.
> ~~She was~~ tired from the months of practice.

$$\downarrow$$

> Sarah Hughes was **happy with her performance in the Olympics but tired from the months of practice.**

108

When the Bushes travel to Washington, ~~they are accompanied by an army of reporters.~~

When they return to Texas, they are accompanied by an army of reporters.

↓

When the Bushes travel to Washington or when they return to Texas, they are accompanied by an army of reporters.

Simple coordination uses familiar COORDINATORS like **and, but,** and **or.** Using these familiar coordinators, you can connect not only words, phrases, and clauses but full sentences as well:

Some species of whales are nearing extinction.

Many countries refuse to accept even a partial ban on whale hunting.

↓

Some species of whales are nearing extinction, **but** many countries refuse to accept even a partial ban on whale hunting.

In 1888, John Boyd Dunlop produced the first pneumatic tire.

A few days later, a bike rider experienced the first flat tire.

↓

In 1888, John Boyd Dunlop produced the first bicycle pneumatic tire, **and** a bike rider experienced the first flat tire just a few days later.

A second and more formal way of coordinating full sentences is by replacing the comma, and usually the coordinator as well, with a semicolon:

There are over 3,000 baseball players in the minor leagues; only about 700 of them will ever reach the majors.

In 1888, John Boyd Dunlop produced the first bicycle pneumatic tire; a bike rider experienced the first flat tire just a few days later.

A third strategy, if you want to make the second sentence clearly command attention, is to separate the two sentences with a period and begin the second with a conjunction:

Some species of whales are nearing extinction. **But** many countries refuse to accept even a partial ban on whale hunting.

In 1888, John Boyd Dunlop produced the first bicycle pneumatic tire. **And** a few days later a bike rider experienced the first flat.

You can vary the effects of simple coordination by interrupting the coordination with a modifier. You put the modifier right after the coordinator and set it off from the rest of the sentence by commas or dashes:

> Some species of whales are nearing extinction. **But, because of the large sums of money at stake,** many countries refuse to accept even a partial ban on whale hunting.

> In 1888, John Boyd Dunlop produced the first bicycle pneumatic tire. **And—as luck would have it—**a bike rider experienced the first flat tire a few days later.

✑ PAIRED COORDINATION

To show a stronger relationship between two words, two phrases, or two clauses, you can use PAIRED COORDINATORS. There are five paired coordinators:

> **both . . . and**
>
> **either . . . or**
>
> **neither . . . nor**
>
> **whether . . . or**
>
> **not only . . . but (also)**

Because their connecting power is greater than that of single coordinators, paired coordinators help to emphasize the connection between the elements they join:

> **Neither** the rain **nor** the sleet
>
> **Whether** to study for the exam **or** party with her friends
>
> **Both** when you exercise **and** how you exercise
>
> **Not only** is Mexican food growing in popularity in the United States, **but** Americans now buy more salsa than ketchup.

Like those with single coordinators, sentences with paired coordinators may be interrupted by modifiers that add details or that help define the writer's attitude. The interruption usually occurs just after the second coordinator of the pair:

> **Not only** is Mexican food growing in popularity in the United States, **but—amazing as it may seem—**Americans now buy more salsa than ketchup.

❧ SERIES COORDINATION

Another coordination pattern is called SERIES COORDINATION, a list of three or more words, phrases, or clauses separated by commas, with a coordinator before the final item in the series:

> Many female moviegoers think Hannibal Lecter is **sexy, dangerous, and irresistible.**

> The inexperienced bobsledders hurtled **down the icy track, over the high-banked curve, and into a snowbank.**

> Sherlock Holmes scrutinized the dead man's mud-caked boots and deduced **where he had lived, how he had been murdered, and when the murder had occurred.**

If they are short, you can even connect sentences with commas and with a final coordinator:

> Many Americans find Hillary Clinton an impressive senator.
>
> She is a caring mother.
>
> She is an accomplished attorney.
>
> She speaks intelligently about important issues.

> Many Americans find Hillary Clinton an impressive senator. **She is a caring mother, she is an accomplished attorney, and she speaks intelligently about important issues.**

Like other patterns, series coordination offers a number of options. You can make the series move slowly and seem lengthy and drawn out, and perhaps even tired, by omitting commas and repeating the coordinator:

> A trip to the supermarket can be a terrible ordeal—**a crowded parking lot and noisy kids and carts that don't go straight and long checkout lines.**

To make the series more rapid and to suggest urgency and excitement, you can eliminate all the coordinators:

> A trip to the supermarket can be a terrible ordeal—**a crowded parking lot, noisy kids, carts that don't go straight, long checkout lines.**

Just as two coordinated structures may be interrupted by a modifier, so may the three or more items of a series:

> Teenagers loved the film *Titanic* because of **the age-old fascination with the disastrous shipwreck, the eye-opening computer-generated**

special effects, and—most especially—the memorably star-crossed lovers played by Leonardo DiCaprio and Kate Winslet.

A series with more than three coordinated words or phrases offers especially interesting opportunities. Instead of lumping items together in a series, as in:

African Americans like Frederick Douglass, W. E. B. DuBois, Zora Neale Hurston, and Malcolm X have written memorable autobiographies.

You can group them into pairs:

African Americans like Frederick Douglass and W. E. B. DuBois, Zora Neale Hurston and Malcolm X, have written memorable autobiographies.

Rather than simply placing the pairs next to one another, you can use prepositions to designate specific relationships between them:

African Americans from Frederick Douglass and W. E. B. DuBois to Zora Neale Hurston and Malcolm X have written memorable autobiographies.

Rhythm and emphasis are important considerations in series coordination. The series, the paired series, and the series with prepositions all create different rhythms. Read each of the sample sentences aloud to see how the different coordination strategies change the sounds and shift emphasis and sense in these series. However the series is arranged, try to order it so that the most important item, if there is one, comes last. Notice that in the examples immediately above, the most recent and prominent African American writers, Zora Neale Hurston and Malcolm X, appear at the end of the series.

✎ USING SUBORDINATION

Let's go back to the two sentences about whales:

Some species of whales are nearing extinction.

Many countries refuse to accept even a partial ban on whale hunting.

With simple coordination, we indicated that these two sentences were equally important:

Some species of whales are nearing extinction, **but** many countries refuse to accept even a partial ban on whale hunting.

If you want to suggest that one of the sentences is less important than the other, you can subordinate one of the sentences:

Although some species of whales are nearing extinction, many countries refuse to accept even a partial ban on whale hunting.

OR

Because many countries refuse to accept even a partial ban on whale hunting, some species of whales are nearing extinction.

By using words such as **although** or **because,** you make the less important sentence into a SUBORDINATE CLAUSE and keep the other as a main clause.

✎ SUBORDINATORS

A subordinate clause is introduced by a SUBORDINATOR, an adverb, or adverb phrase that relates the meaning of the subordinate clause to the meaning of the main clause. Here is a list of subordinators which can help you specify contrast, cause, time, place, condition, and degree:

Contrast:	**Although**
	Even though
	While
Cause:	**Because**
	Since
	As
Time:	**When**
	Whenever
	While
	Once
	Before
	After
	Since
	Until
	As long as
	As soon as
Place:	**Where**
	Wherever

Condition: **If**
               When
               Provided that
               In case
               Assuming that

Negative
condition: **Unless**

Alternative
condition: **Whether or not**

Degree: **Inasmuch as**
               Insofar as
               To the extent that

As this partial list suggests, you often have a choice among several subordinators. To indicate a time relationship between these two clauses:

The Mongol invaders threatened to conquer all of Europe.

Then Genghis Khan's death forced them to return to Asia.

you may choose among the subordinators **until, before,** and **just when,** and you may subordinate one or the other clause:

Just when the Mongol invaders threatened to conquer all of Europe, Genghis Khan's death forced them to return to Asia.

OR

The Mongol invaders threatened to conquer all of Europe **until Genghis Khan's death forced them to return to Asia.**

Even when the meaning commits you to subordinating one sentence and not the other, you may still have a choice among subordinators:

Michelangelo's *Pietà* was damaged by a madman.

Museum officials display it behind a protective glass shield.

Because
Since   } **Michelangelo's *Pietà* was damaged by a madman,** museum officials display(ed) it
After   behind a glass shield.

Any one of these subordinators is appropriate in this sentence because each logically links the step taken by the museum officials to protect the sculpture (the result) to the madman's act (the cause). But there is a difference between the subordinators. **Because** emphasizes the cause, **after** emphasizes the time sequence (first the damage, then the protection), and **since** gives roughly equal emphasis to cause and time sequence.

✌ POSITIONING SUBORDINATE CLAUSES

In the sentences about Michelangelo's *Pietà*, the subordinate clauses come before the main clause. But subordinate clauses may also occur either at the end or in the middle of sentences. You can control the emphasis and meaning of your sentences by varying where you place subordinate clauses. Look at these two sentences:

> **If local residents are willing to put up with them,** nuclear plants can provide cheap energy and enrich an area's economy.
>
> OR
>
> Nuclear plants can provide cheap energy and enrich an area's economy, **if local residents are willing to put up with them.**

Since a sentence tends to impress on the reader what it says toward the end, where the stress naturally falls, the first example sentence implies that nuclear plants are desirable; the second version implies a grimmer view, directing attention less to the plants' economic advantages than to the residents' concern for safety.

You can also change emphasis and rhythm with different punctuation. A dash, instead of a comma, lengthens the pause and places greater emphasis on *if*, adding to the reader's uneasiness:

> Nuclear plants can provide cheap energy and enrich an area's economy—**if local residents are willing to put up with them.**

✌ SUBORDINATION IN CONTEXT

As we suggest in the previous section, where you position a subordinate clause within your sentence depends on what you choose to emphasize and the rhythm you choose to produce. Where you position a subordinate clause also depends on the surrounding sentences. The reverse is true as well: the sentence you choose for your main clause and the one you choose for your subordinate clause will affect the sentences that come before and after them. Let's look at two sentences about the aftermath of the World Trade Center disaster to illustrate how sentences affect one another:

The World Trade Center disaster curbed America's desire for building skyscrapers.

Architects in Asia and Europe are developing sky-high projects.

↓

Although the World Trade Center disaster curbed America's desire for building skyscrapers, architects in Asia and Europe are developing sky-high projects.

OR

Though architects in Asia and Europe are developing sky-high projects, the World Trade Center disaster curbed America's desire for building skyscrapers.

In the first combined sentence, the main clause focuses on the "sky-high projects" in Asia and Europe, so the reader expects that the next few sentences will continue that discussion. They might name some of the countries or discuss their individual building project. In the second combined sentence, the main clause focuses on the curbing of America's desire for tall buildings. Here the reader expects the next few sentences to discuss that curbed desire, maybe by exploring some of the projects that have been discontinued in American cities.

The choice of which sentence to subordinate is an important one, as you can see, because it can determine the direction of the rest of a paragraph or essay.

☙ SIMPLIFYING SUBORDINATE CLAUSES

Subordination is a helpful way to indicate how your ideas are related, but subordination can make your sentences wordy unless you're careful. A subordinate clause with the same subject as the main clause can sometimes be simplified to a more concise phrase. When you spot a word like *is, are, was,* or *were* in a subordinate clause, take it as an invitation to eliminate unnecessary words:

Although ~~they were~~ common a hundred years ago, red wolves no longer populate our woods in significant numbers.

Although common a hundred years ago, red wolves no longer populate our woods in significant numbers.

☙ USING SUBORDINATION AND COORDINATION TOGETHER

Coordination and subordination are so common that you'll often have opportunities to use them together in the same sentence. When you use them together, you can revise the subordination or coordination patterns in exactly the same ways as when you use them alone:

Thoreau portrayed himself as a contemplative observer of nature.

He also appears cantankerous, competitive, and even selfish, spending more than half of *Walden* ranting about how stupidly other people live.

↓

While Thoreau portrayed himself as a contemplative observer of nature, he also appears cantankerous, competive, and even selfish, spending more than half of *Walden* ranting about how stupidly other people live.

OR

Thoreau portrayed himself as a contemplative observer of nature, **though he also appears cantankerous and competitive and even selfish, spending more than half of *Walden* ranting about how stupidly other people live.**

OR

Thoreau portrayed himself as a contemplative observer of nature. **But he also appears cantankerous, competitive, even selfish, spending more than half of *Walden* ranting about how stupidly other people live.**

OR

Thoreau **not only** portrayed himself as a contemplative observer of nature **but also** appears cantankerous, competitive, and even selfish—spending more than half of *Walden* ranting about how stupidly other people live.

✍ PLAYING WITH COORDINATION AND SUBORDINATION

The exercises provide opportunities to play with coordinate and subordinate structures, constructing them, moving them around, and using them to write economically and to focus your sentences and paragraphs. When you're drafting or revising papers of your own, remember to look for opportunities to use coordination and subordination creatively. The creative use of these common structures can help you focus as well as add rhythm and emphasis to your writing.

EXERCISES

Using Patterns of Coordination and Subordination

I. Coordination. Revise each of the following groups of sentences into a single sentence by using one or more of the patterns of coordination: simple coordination, paired coordinators, or series coordinators.

EXAMPLE

New Hampshire is the only state that does not have a general sales tax. And New Hampshire is the only state that does not have an income tax.

New Hampshire is the only state without **either** a general sales tax **or** an income tax.

OR

New Hampshire is the only state that has **neither a** general sales tax **nor** an income tax.

A. **1.** All the filmmakers who worked on the movie *Smoke Signals* were Native Americans.

2. All the performers in the movie *Smoke Signals* were Native Americans.

3. All the crew members on the movie *Smoke Signals* were Native Americans.

4. The director and screenwriter of the movie *Smoke Signals* were Native Americans.

B. **1.** You can usually recognize the villains of cartoon adventure programs in two ways.

2. The villains laugh fiendishly.

3. The villains speak with foreign accents.

C. **1.** Cave diving is incredibly terrifying.

2. It is exhilarating.

D. **1.** The viewers of pantomime are aided by the supple mind of the actor.

    2. The viewers of pantomime are aided by the supple body of the actor.

    3. The viewers of pantomime can see what is not there.

    4. The viewers of pantomime can hear what is not said.

    5. The viewers of pantomime can believe the impossible.

E. **1.** The specific fruits that Wrigley uses to make Juicy Fruit gum remain a closely guarded secret.

    2. The fruit flavorings probably include lemon.

    3. The fruit flavorings probably include orange.

    4. The fruit flavorings probably include pineapple.

    5. The fruit flavorings most definitely include banana.

II. Subordination. Revise each sequence of sentences below into a single sentence by converting one or more of the original sentences into a subordinate clause. For several of the sequences, write more than one version. You may want to review the list of subordinators in this chapter.

EXAMPLE

Many Americans use their microwaves to make popcorn. The Iroquois Indians used heated sand to pop theirs.

Although many Americans use their microwaves to make popcorn, the Iroquois Indians used heated sand to pop theirs.

OR

While many Americans use their microwaves to make popcorn, the Iroquois Indians used heated sand to pop theirs.

F. **1.** Giant Amazon water lilies range up to seven feet across.

    2. Giant Amazon water lilies are large enough to provide living space for insects, birds, and lizards.

G. **1.** The United States spends more money on medical care than any country on earth.

    2. The United States has more spectacular medical technology than any country on earth.

   3. The United States has one of the highest ratios of doctors and hospitals to people.

   4. Nevertheless, the United States lags behind several European countries in reducing infant mortality rates and extending life expectancy.

H. **1.** The Western world continues to regard acupuncture with suspicion.

   2. Perhaps the reason is that acupuncture is so alien to our own concept of medical treatment.

I. **1.** Halle Berry and Denzel Washington won Academy Awards in 2002.

   2. It was the first time two African American actors won Oscars in the same year.

J. **1.** Elvis changed American music.

   2. He successfully blended R&B, rock, and country-western.

Bargains and Barbies and Junky Old Toasters

Using subordination and coordination whenever possible, revise the sentences below into an amusing narrative about garage sales. Not every sentence will contain either coordination or subordination; you'll be able to make other structures as well. If you're familiar with garage sales, add details that will make the narrative more vivid and lifelike.

1. "Get up, Jenny," Mom would call on Saturday mornings.

2. "We've got to get going."

3. "Or we'll miss the bargains."

4. Mom dragged me to every garage sale in town.

5. This happened most of my childhood.

6. She'd get to them early.

7. And she'd pick through the lamps.

8. She'd pick through the toasters.

9. She'd pick through the coffeemakers.

10. She'd pick through the couches.

11. She was looking for bargains.

12. She picked.

13. She talked to the other women who followed the sales.

14. At the same time, I'd scrounge through boxes of games.

15. And I'd scrounge through boxes of toys.

16. I was looking for Barbies.

17. And I was looking for Barbie clothes to add to my collection.

18. Mom hardly ever found bargains.

19. "Junk," she usually said.

20. She said this as we got into the Toyota and headed for the next sale.

21. Mom used the sales to see her friends.

22. And Mom used the sales to learn about our neighbors.

23. At the same time, I built the best Barbie collection in town.

Revising Patterns of Coordination and Subordination

I. Make each of the following sentences more effective by revising the patterns of coordination.

EXAMPLE

Activities at the Oatmeal Festival in Oatmeal, Texas, include an over-ripe cantaloupe toss along with a cowchip kickoff and an oatmeal-box-stacking contest and even an oatmeal sculpture competition.

Activities at the the Oatmeal Festival in Oatmeal, Texas, include **not only** an overripe cantaloupe toss and a cowchip kickoff **but also** an oatmeal-box-stacking contest and an oatmeal sculpture competition.

A. More people live by themselves, and more women work, and more money is available, and for these reasons, one of every three U.S. food dollars now goes to restaurants or fast-food places.

B. In the elusiveness of the enemy and the widespread drug use among our troops, Vietnam differed from all earlier American wars; it differed in the American soldiers' sense of outrage.

C. *South Park* may have been the most unusual TV cartoon series ever shown because it employed amateurish drawings of little kids and it lovingly emphasized vulgar language, questionable behavior, and violent death. Not only that, it also delivered a memorably sophisticated satire of American culture.

D. New York City may be the art capital of the world. New York City may not be the art capital of the world. It is definitely home to some of the most important art museums in the United States.

E. Spike Lee's film *Do the Right Thing* offered genuine insight into the rage behind the Los Angeles riots of 1992, and John Singleton's film *Boyz N the Hood* offered genuine insight into the rage behind the Los Angeles riots of 1992.

II. Revise each pair of sentences below into a single sentence by converting one of the original sentences into a subordinate clause; then reduce the clause to a phrase.

EXAMPLE

  1. You are traveling in Scotland.

  2. Then you surely want to visit the city of St. Andrews and its famous golf course.

$$\downarrow$$

When you are traveling in Scotland, you surely want to visit the city of St. Andrews and its famous golf course.

OR

When traveling in Scotland, you surely want to visit the city of St. Andrews and its famous golf course.

F. **1.** You are denied credit.

  2. Then you are entitled to an explanation.

G. **1.** They were just a handful of men and women.

  2. Still, American transcendentalists (like Ralph Waldo Emerson and Margaret Fuller) exerted a powerful influence in the nineteenth century.

H. **1.** Shakespeare's King Lear was unable to tell the difference between true love and false love.

  2. For this reason, he lost his kingdom and eventually his life.

I. **1.** They were once deserted during the summer months.

  2. Ski resorts have now created popular warm-weather attractions, like the Alpine slide.

J.   **1.** You are at the J. Lo concert.

2. Then turn off your cell phone.

No More Burgers

Use coordination and subordination to revise the sentences below into an essay that persuades the reader of the need for shifting to a vegetarian diet. Use reasons and examples of your own whenever you choose. Add details for vividness, and change whatever you feel will improve the paragraph and make it more convincing. Not every sentence will contain either coordination or subordination; you'll be able to use other strategies as well.

1. Meat eaters have usually regarded vegetarians as emaciated fanatics.

2. The fanatics pick at a few leaves, nuts, and berries.

3. These fastidious leaf lovers may know something that most steak lovers don't want to know.

4. Populations continue to grow.

5. Available land dwindles rapidly.

6. As these occur, there will be less and less food for the world's hungry mouths.

7. Vegetarian diets encourage wiser use of our animal resources.

8. Vegetarian diets encourage wiser use of our land.

9. For these reasons, we should shift to basically vegetarian diets.

10. We must make this shift.

11. Without it, we face hunger.

12. The hunger is massive.

13. The hunger is global.

14. Here is a startling example.

15. A steer weighs 1,100 pounds.

16. A steer devours almost three tons of nutrients during its life.

17. The steer yields only 460 pounds of edible meat.

18. This means that the steer must gobble up over 12 pounds of food for every pound of its own edible meat.

19. This becomes clear, then.

20. We can feed more people with corn than with sirloins.

21. We can feed more people with lentils than with T-bones.

22. We can feed more people with soybeans than with rib eyes.

23. In addition to the points above, we don't need all that meat for nutrition.

24. Even the World Health Organization acknowledges [this].

25. Properly combined, meatless meals supply all the nutrients essential to the human diet.

26. A fresh fruit salad is a meatless meal.

27. A catch-of-the-day rainbow trout is a meatless meal.

28. Hot vegetable soup is a meatless meal.

29. Swiss cheese fondue is a meatless meal.

30. They are also nutritious meals.

31. All indications suggest that meatless meals provide plenty of nutrition.

32. They do so at lower cost.

33. They do so with more economic use of the land.

34. It may be some time before famines force us to do something.

35. Nonetheless, we may have to sacrifice burgers for broccoli.

36. We may have to serve spaghetti without meatballs.

37. While this is true, it is not too soon to start retraining our taste buds right now.

38. Anyone for eggplant casserole?

Using Patterns of Coordination and Subordination in Context

Strengthen each paragraph below by using coordination where appropriate or by revising one or more of the original sentences into a subordinate clause. Try to make the paragraph more concise and more sharply focused.

EXAMPLE

Hershey's once called its candy bar the "Great American Chocolate Bar." And Hershey, Pennsylvania, may just be the Great American Small Town. It has clean, tree-lined streets, and it has magnificent gardens. You can also find museums and a seventy-six-acre amusement park, not to mention a school for underprivileged children. The aroma from the chocolate factory is pervasive. For this reason, there is no pollution to smell. Founded by candy magnate Milton Snavely Hershey, the little paradise reportedly has no jail. It does not have poverty. It has a definite surplus of chocolate. For sure.

Hershey's once called its candy bar the "Great American Chocolate Bar." And Hershey, Pennsylvania, may just be the Great American Small Town. It **not only** has clean, tree-lined streets, **but** it **also** has magnificent gardens. You can also find museums and a seventy-six-acre amusement park, not to mention a school for underprivileged children. **Because the aroma from the chocolate factory is pervasive,** there is no pollution to smell. Founded by candy magnate Milton Snavely Hershey, the little paradise reportedly has no jail **and** no poverty, **but** it has a definite surplus of chocolate. For sure.

A. More and more teachers moonlight because they cannot make it on their regular income. They are victims of declining pay scales and the lack of public support for their efforts. According to one expert, teachers have only two choices. One choice is that they can leave teaching. The other is that they can find second jobs to supplement their income. Many teachers have found their other jobs to be lucrative and enjoyable. For this reason, they are taking the first alternative and resigning. And those who leave the teaching profession are often the best. They are the type schools can least afford to lose.

B. Scientists can't explain why temperatures in Antarctica have climbed measurably in the past fifty years. The results are obvious. There is more snow. There is less sea ice. There are fewer penguins.

C. She's a slob. You're a neatnik. He demands quiet all the time. You like loud music and TV. Perhaps you can't get along with your roommate. Then university housing officials suggest you communicate openly, honestly, and immediately, as problems arise. Still can't make peace between yourselves? Then let a dorm adviser mediate between the two of you. Or ask for a transfer to another room. You should ask for a transfer if the conflict persists.

Wrestling Mania

Use coordination and subordination to revise the sentences below into an essay which persuades its readers that professional wrestling is consumed with violence and sex. Not every sentence will contain either coordination or subordination; you'll be able to make other structures as well. Add details for vividness, and change whatever you feel will improve the paragraph and make it more convincing.

1. Before cable television, professional wrestling pitted big sweaty good guys against big hairy bad guys.

2. This happened in wholesome but violent morality plays.

3. Hardly anyone watched it.

4. Cable television transformed wrestling into a violent mix.

5. The mix is composed of comic book and soap opera.

6. Now it is often watched by millions of fans.

7. Traditional wrestling is an athletic contest.

8. Professional wrestling is more about story than sport.

9. Professional wrestling is more about exhibitionism than sport.

10. The wrestlers are steroid-pumped giants.

11. The wrestlers grab their crotches.

12. They give the finger.

13. They partake in simulated sex.

14. And they partake in mock Satan worship.

15. The wrestlers follow a script that determines who will win and how.

16. So who are the fans for these over-the-top displays of staged violence?

17. Surveys indicate [this].

18. Adolescent boys make up much of the viewing audience.

19. Preteens make up much of the viewing audience.

20. Teens make up much of the viewing audience.

21. But lots of others enjoy the spectacle.

22. It consists of grown men and women in face makeup and tights.

23. They are bashing chairs over each other's heads.

24. They are throwing their opponents into screaming audiences.

25. And it doesn't hurt that matches are packed with excessive violence.

26. Matches are packed with gratuitous sexual references.

27. Matches are packed with enough exploited hot bodies to fill a Roman coliseum.

Noun Substitutes

Preview

This unit introduces you to four structures that substitute for simple nouns: infinitives, gerunds, that clauses, and wh- clauses. You create infinitives and gerunds by changing verb forms. You generally add **to** in order to make a verb into an infinitive and **-ing** to make it into a gerund. Infinitives, gerunds, and noun clauses can help you tie loosely related sentences together more tightly. And when you balance them or put them in a series, noun substitutes can add sophistication to your writing. Noun substitutes come in handy when you need to revise a vague *this, which,* or *it* or a series of loosely connected sentences.

❧ TYPES OF NOUN SUBSTITUTES

When you're writing quickly to produce an early draft, you sometimes state an observation in a single clause or sentence and then comment on it with the next. To relate the two clauses, you might refer to one with a pronoun like **this, that,** or **it:**

1. You could deposit nuclear waste in outer space. **This** would be one way to solve a difficult dilemma.
2. Some people blame all social problems on moral decay. **That** is a gross oversimplification.
3. Laura was late for her trial, and **it** made the judge furious.
4. Why don't more Americans listen to classical music? **This** is a mystery to Europeans.

When a pronoun refers to a whole clause, the relationship between the clause and the pronoun is generally vague. To make relationships between statements clearer and more specific, you can replace words like **this, that,** and **it** by combining the two sentences and converting one of them into a NOUN SUBSTITUTE: a gerund phrase, an infinitive phrase, a that clause, or a wh- clause.

In Example 1, you can revise the first sentence into a GERUND PHRASE:

~~You could~~ deposit nuclear waste in outer space. **This** would be one way to solve a difficult dilemma.

↓

Depositing nuclear waste in outer space would be one way to solve a difficult dilemma.

In Example 2, you can revise the first sentence into an INFINITIVE PHRASE:

~~Some people~~ blame all social problems on moral decay. **That** is a gross oversimplification.

↓

To blame all social problems on moral decay is a gross oversimplification.

In Example 3, you can revise the first sentence into a THAT CLAUSE:

Laura was late for her trial, and **it** really made the judge furious.

↓

That Laura was late for her trial really made the judge furious.

In Example 4, you can revise the question into a WH- CLAUSE:

Why don't more Americans listen to classical music? **This** is a mystery to Europeans.

↓

Why more Americans don't listen to classical music is a mystery to Europeans.

Infinitives, gerunds, that clauses, and wh- clauses retain the meaning they had as full sentences. By combining them with other sentences, you specify relationships between the separate ideas.

❧ CONTRUCTING INFINITIVES AND GERUNDS

To make a gerund phrase, you change the verb in a clause to an **-ing** form. For instance, in the following example you can make the verbs *smoke* and *cooks* into **smoking** and **cooking:**

~~You~~ smoke cigarettes.

This is dangerous to your health.

Smoking cigarettes is dangerous to your health.

~~Philip~~ cooks with tofu.

Philip loves **this**.

Philip loves **cooking with tofu.**

Sometimes when you make a sentence into a gerund phrase, you turn the original subject into a possessive form, like **dog's** in the next example:

The neighbors complained about **this**.

The dog howled and whined.

The neighbors complained about **the dog's howling and whining.**

Just as you can convert a clause into a gerund phrase, you can also convert a clause into an infinitive phrase by changing the verb form. To make a verb into an infinitive, you usually add the word *to*. In the following example, the verb *surround* becomes the infinitive **to surround:**

~~Many gardeners~~ surround their gardens with wire fencing.

~~It~~ is the best way for farmers to prevent rabbits from eating their vegetables.

To surround their gardens with wire fencing is the best way for farmers to prevent rabbits from eating their vegetables.

When you change a clause into an infinitive phrase, you can sometimes keep the subject of the verb by placing the subject after the word *for*, as in the next example:

A restaurant earns five stars.

This means it has superior food and service.

For a restaurant to earn five stars means it has superior food and service.

Sometimes you have the choice of revising a clause into either a gerund phrase or an infinitive phrase, according to which sounds best to you:

Venus Williams likes **this**.

~~She~~ plays tennis.

Venus Williams likes **playing tennis**.

OR

Venus Williams likes **to play tennis**.

✍ CONSTRUCTING NOUN CLAUSES

Noun clauses occur in two basic varieties: that clauses and wh- clauses. To turn a sentence into a that clause, you put the word *that* in front of it:

E.T. said **this**.

He really needed to phone home.

E.T. said **that he really needed to phone home**.

Personal computers did not exist until 1978.

This is hard to believe.

That personal computers did not exist until 1978 is hard to believe.

There are two kinds of wh- clauses; they correspond to the two kinds of questions in English. The first kind of question can be answered with "yes" or "no." For example:

Did the Dow Jones stock averages drop yesterday?

To make a yes–no question into a wh- clause, you first convert the question into a statement and then you add **whether** or **whether or not** in front:

The reporter asked the president **this**.

Would taxes be cut again this year?

The reporter asked the **president whether taxes would be cut again this year**.

You have to answer the second kind of question with more than "yes" or "no." This kind of question is introduced by a word such as **when, why, what,** or **how,** as in:

When is payday?

To make the second kind of question into a wh- clause, you use one of the following words:

what

where, wherever

who, whoever

when, whenever

whom, whomever

why

whose

how, how much, however

which, whichever

Here are some examples of wh- clauses made from the second kind of question:

Many Kansans know **this**.

What is it like to live though a tornado?

Many Kansans know **what it is like to live through a tornado**.

The Gulf War made the public realize **this**.

How dependent are we on Middle Eastern nations for oil?

The Gulf War made the public realize **how dependent we are on Middle Eastern nations for oil**.

What began as the tinkering of two hackers in a suburban garage?

It became the Apple Computer Company.

What began as the tinkering of two hackers in a suburban garage became the Apple Computer Company.

✢ REARRANGING NOUN SUBSTITUTES

You can often strengthen sentences by rearranging noun substitutes. Sometimes putting a that clause into a subject position makes a sentence front-heavy and awkward, as in the sentence about computers:

That personal computers did not exist until 1978 is hard to believe.

In this case, you can revise the sentence by moving the clause to the end of the sentence and placing an **it** in the subject position:

It is hard to believe **that personal computers did not exist until 1978.**

You can move infinitive phrases from the subject position in the same way, by adding an **it** in the subject position:

To marry in June is traditional.

↓

It is traditional **to marry in June.**

So if a sentence seems front-heavy because of a long clause or infinitive phrase, move the structure to the end of the sentence.

∾ ACHIEVING BALANCE AND PARALLELISM WITH NOUN SUBSTITUTES

You can make your writing appear more sophisticated and under control if you use balanced noun substitutes. Notice how much stronger the following sentence is when you make the first subordinate clause, *you support gender equality in the armed forces,* into a gerund phrase to balance the second gerund phrase:

You support gender equality in the armed forces by viewing women as fit for combat.

↓

Supporting gender equality in the armed forces means **viewing women as fit for combat.**

When you balance structures, you generally say that one thing is like another. But balancing sometimes implies a comparison, as in the next sentence, which suggests how great a golfer Tiger Woods is by comparing him to the greatest English poet:

To say that Tiger Woods plays golf is **to say that Shakespeare scribbled.**

Just as you can often strengthen a sentence by balancing noun substitutes, you can often strengthen longer stretches of writing with noun substitutes in a series. The following draft is loosely constructed because the structure of the sentences doesn't emphasize how closely related their ideas are:

> Registered nurses (RNs) are highly educated professionals. Most states require RNs to complete a two-, three-, or four-year education. Then the nurses must pass a state RN licensing exam. And RNs must earn continuing-education credits in order to renew their licenses.

But the revision, which turns the loosely connected sentences into the balanced infinitive phrases **to complete a two-, three-, or four-year education, to pass a state RN licensing exam,** and **to earn continuing-education credits . . . ,** shows the close relationship among the separate ideas. The revision drives home the point clearly and forcefully by building on the rhythm of the infinitive series:

> Nurses are highly educated professionals. Most states require RNs **to complete a two-, three-, or four-year education, to pass a state RN licensing exam, and to earn continuing-education credits in order to renew their licenses.**

You can achieve similar results with a series of that clauses:

> Nurses are highly educated professionals. Most states require **that RNs complete a two-, three-, or four-year education, that they pass a state RN licensing exam, and that they earn continuing-education credits in order to renew their licenses.**

Sentence components exist in relation to other parts within their own sentences and in relation to other sentences as well. That's why it's important to read your own texts carefully, listening to and planning how to balance components and make them fit together into larger, more thoughtful, more pleasing sequences.

❧ PLAYING WITH NOUN SUBSTITUTES

The exercises provide opportunities to play with gerunds, infinitives, and noun clauses, constructing them, moving them around, and using them to write economically and to better tie your sentences and paragraphs together. When you're drafting or revising papers of your own, remember to look for opportunities to use noun substitutes creatively. The point of all the sentence-combining exercises is for you to improve your own writing.

EXERCISES

Constructing Noun Substitutes

Revise each sequence below into a single sentence using gerunds or infinitives in Sentences A–E and either that clauses or wh- clauses in Sentences F–J. You can make more than one version for some of the sequences.

EXAMPLE I: GERUNDS OR INFINITIVES

Millions of people have begun [this].

~~They~~ garden for relaxation and exercise.

Millions of people have begun **to garden for relaxation and exercise.**

OR

Millions of people have begun **gardening for relaxation and exercise.**

A. **1.** ~~You can~~ bury a dead cat at midnight.

    2. ~~Or you can~~ rub the spot with grasshopper spit.

    3. [This] might cure warts as effectively as medical treatment.

B. **1.** ~~Someone~~ says [this].

    2. History is a record of dates and battles.

    3. [This] ignores most of history's significance.

C. **1.** Because it's a fruit, not a vegetable, [this] can be tricky.

    2. ~~You~~ classify the tomato.

D. **1.** ~~You~~ reduce your weight.

    2. [It] is not just a matter of [this].

    3. ~~You~~ clip a diet from a magazine.

E. **1.** Swindlers love [this].

    2. ~~They~~ find suckers who dream of quick profits.

EXAMPLE II: THAT CLAUSES OR WH- CLAUSES

That clause

The earth's climate may be changing rapidly because of industrial pollution.

Scientists and environmentalists recognize [this].

Scientists and environmentalists recognize **that the earth's climate may be changing rapidly because of industrial pollution.**

Wh- clause

Too many children know [this].

What is it like to grow up with parents who hate each other?

Too many children know **what it is like to grow up with parents who hate each other.**

F.   1. Health clubs nationwide are betting [this].

   2. Boxing aerobics—a blend of boxing moves and aerobic dance steps—will attract men into aerobics class.

G.   1. What do the Olympics Games boil down to?

   2. [This] is a world-class event for athletes and world-class business for commercial sponsors.

H.   1. Should prisoners be used for medical experiments?

   2. [This] is not only a legal question but a moral question as well.

I.   1. Social unfairness is [this].

   2. What justifies government affirmative action programs?

J.   1. Television still considers men more competent.

   2. If you want to prove [this], just count how few news anchor teams consist of two women.

Saving the Forests, Saving Ourselves

Using gerunds, infinitives, and that clauses where appropriate, revise the following sentences into a paragraph that explains why we must save the rain forests.

Not every sentence will contain a noun substitute; you'll be able to make other structures as well.

1. Nowhere is life more abundant than in tropical rain forests.

2. Or nowhere is life more threatened than in tropical rain forests.

3. Rain forests supply material resources for developed nations.

4. And rain forests supply agricultural land for undeveloped nations.

5. So we burn the forests down at a feverish pace.

6. And we hack the forests down at a feverish pace.

7. In the past, [this] was easy.

8. We considered the loss of forest land as the price for progress.

9. But now, scientists, government officials, and ordinary citizens recognize [this].

10. Rain forests are fragile environments.

11. [This] and [this] destroy animals and plants.

12. You cut down rain forests.

13. You burn rain forests.

14. Animals and plants can't be renewed.

15. Suppose we continue [it].

16. We destroy forests at the present pace.

17. Then we will damage the atmosphere.

18. And we will wipe out sources for new medicines to cure AIDS, cancer, and diabetes.

19. We have finally learned [this].

20. The welfare of our planet is clearly linked to the welfare of the rain forests.

Creating Noun Substitutes

Revise each of the following sentences by replacing the pronoun in boldface with a gerund, an infinitive, a that clause, or a wh- clause. In sentences where the pronoun is *it*, you have the additional option of keeping it and inserting the noun substitute elsewhere in the sentence. Try experimenting with different kinds of noun substitutes.

EXAMPLE

It proved to be a memorable technological achievement.

It proved to be a memorable technological achievement **for NASA to land the Pathfinder rocket on Mars.**

OR

Landing the Pathfinder rocket on Mars proved to be a memorable technological achievement for NASA.

OR

What NASA did when it landed the Pathfinder rocket on Mars was a memorable technological achievement.

A. **This** is a good example of Americans' growing concern about the environment.

B. **It** threatened to endanger our relationship.

C. What none of us could understand was **this.**

D. You should have decided **that** before you mailed the letter.

E. **This** can be a difficult task for some people.

Trail of Tears

Using gerunds, infinitives, and that clauses where they are appropriate, revise the following sentences into a draft that explains how the infamous Cherokee Trail of Tears was named. Not every sentence will contain a noun substitute; you'll be able to make other structures as well.

1. For over forty-five years the Cherokees in Georgia had existed as an independent republic.

2. Then prospectors discovered valuable minerals and gold on the Native Americans' territory.

3. This discovery made land speculators grow interested in [this].

4. They acquired the Cherokees' land.

5. Over 16,000 Cherokees were compelled to [this].

6. They abandoned their property, livestock, and belongings in Georgia in 1838.

7. In the dead of winter, the Cherokees were relocated 900 miles west to Indian Territory.

8. This caused much hardship.

9. The Cherokees were escorted by 10,000 armed soldiers.

10. The soldiers rode on horseback.

11. At the same time, the Cherokees walked.

12. Disease, malnutrition, and exposure killed more than 4,000 Cherokees during the march.

13. At first, the Cherokees buried their dead where they fell.

14. Such frequent burials caused delays.

15. So the soldiers allowed burials only once every three days.

16. All the Cherokees wanted was [this].

17. They bury their loved ones.

18. Instead, the survivors had to carry their dead until the appointed burial days.

19. This added to their anguish.

20. Some Cherokees said [this].

21. Their tragic journey was "the trail where they cried."

22. Others called it the Trail of Tears.

23. By either name, this was a forced migration long remembered for its brutality.

Revising with Noun Substitutes

Revise each of the following sentences to make the most effective use of gerunds, infinitives, that clauses, and wh- clauses. Rearrange the parts of your sentence when necessary.

EXAMPLE

Spain, which has seventeen distinctive cooking regions, is loved by culinary experts for that reason.

↓

What culinary experts love about Spain is that it has seventeen different cooking regions.

A. Solar power is all about one thing; it converts the sun's energy into electricity.

B. If you use the lap-shoulder belt, studies show that this will reduce the chance that you will be killed in a car crash by 60 percent.

C. You can contribute to the conscience fund of the U.S. Treasury Department, which is one way that citizens who suffer second thoughts about cheating on their tax returns can soothe their consciences.

D. Getting their children into college used to be the goal of millions of Americans; nowadays, with the spiraling costs of higher education, it has become a bigger challenge to pay for college.

E. People doze at the wheel, and this is the major reason that motorists run off the road and hit parked vehicles, according to a national study involving 2,000 accidents.

Road Warrior

Revise the following sentences into a final draft which explains how Henry Ford's Model T shaped our world. Not every sentence will contain a noun substitute; you'll be able to make other structures as well. If you can, add details for vividness.

1. It took Henry Ford's Model T, the "Tin Lizzie."

2. It changed America's cultural life.

3. It changed America's social life.

4. It changed America's economic life.

5. The Model T was a lightweight car.

6. It was a powerful car.

7. It boasted a 20-hp engine.

8. It boasted a two-speed transmission.

9. And it was affordable.

10. This was more than anything else.

11. Cars were luxuries for the wealthy.

12. This was until Ford made the Model T in 1908.

13. Other cars cost $5,000.

14. The Model T cost just $850.

15. Its price went down almost every year.

16. Ford produced them cheaply

17. The reason was he made full use of the assembly line.

18. In 1914, 13,000 Ford workers produced 260,720 cars.

19. It took over 66,000 U.S. autoworkers.

20. They produced 286,770 cars for Ford's competitors.

21. In 1909, Henry Ford said, "I'm going to democratize the automobile."

22. He did.

23. They bought cars.

24. [This] became a middle-class ritual.

25. Ford sold 15 million Model T's before [this].

26. Ford ended production in 1927.

27. The car for the multitudes created the car culture.

28. The Model T created the modern economy.

29. It built the oil industry.

30. It built the steel industry.

31. It built the rubber industry.

32. The growing number of drivers demanded better roads and services.

33. Gas stations sprang up on roads and highways.

34. Motels sprang up on roads and highways.

35. Restaurants sprang up on roads and highways.

36. We have the Lizzie to thank for [this].

37. What does our country look like today?

38. Ford's little car conquered the world.

PART Three

LESSONS IN REARRANGEMENT: REVISING WHOLE DRAFTS

Coherence

Preview

The main point of this lesson is that when you revise, you have to think about how to guide your readers from one sentence to the next and from one paragraph to another. When you provide the links between such structures, your writing has coherence. Strategies that can help you achieve coherence include the use of connectives and connective phrases; reference to a previously stated word or phrase by repetition, pronouns, or synonyms; and the arrangement of sentences into patterns, including the proper ordering of old and new information. You can use these same strategies to help connect your paragraphs.

✌ THE WRITER AS TOUR GUIDE

Writing is a little like guiding a group on a tour. When you lead a tour, you need to talk about how individual stops along the way relate to one another, or your tour group will feel jerked from one place to the next instead of experiencing a smooth journey between landmarks. When you write, you need to make your readers see how your sentences relate to one another so that they feel they have gone on a smooth journey instead of being jerked about. Look at the three sentences below, for example:

> Many people exercise every day and never lose weight. Exercising is important. The only sure way to lose weight is to eat less.

The sentences seem to make a contrast between exercise, eating less, and losing weight. But they don't make the contrast clear. That's because they lack a connective word or phrase that would smoothly link one sentence to the other and make clear the precise relationship between exercising, losing weight, and eating less. The two versions below include those connectives:

> Many people exercise every day and never lose weight. Exercising is important. **Still,** the only sure way to lose weight is to eat less.

> OR

> Many people exercise every day and never lose weight. **No doubt** exercising is important, **but** the only sure way to lose weight is to eat less.

The connectives **still** and **no doubt . . . but** in these two versions link the three ideas by highlighting the contrast between the two weight loss approaches. By linking the ideas, the connectives move readers from sentence to sentence without disruption. When the ideas in sentences and paragraphs are clearly linked to one another, a passage has COHERENCE.

Writers generally pay closer attention to the coherence of their paragraphs when they reach the revising stage of the writing process. It's easy to understand why you might draft a paragraph that isn't as coherent as it could be: often as you draft, your full attention is on generating ideas that will help you move your discussion along. You want to get all of the ideas down on paper and in the most effective order, so you jump from idea to idea, not always smoothing over the small jumps you're making. When you revise, however, you want to eliminate those gaps and make your readers' journey through your draft a smoother one.

Let's look more closely at the three major strategies you can use to link sentences to one another within paragraphs and across paragraph boundaries: (1) using connective words and phrases; (2) referring to earlier words and phrases (by repetition, through synonyms, and through pronouns); and (3) arranging sentences into structural patterns, including the proper ordering of old and new information.

❧ USING CONNECTIVES

Connective Words

Sometimes the logical connection between sentences is so obvious that you don't need to signal it with a connective. The relationship between the next two sentences is straightforward. The second sentence clearly gives three examples to illustrate the generalization in the first sentence:

> Most people can learn the basics of even a complex craft quickly. In just weeks, they can learn **to carve, weave, or embroider.**

Adding a connective like **for example** to such a passage in order to directly state the relationship is probably unnecessary.

But whenever the connection between two sentences is not obvious, you can provide a link between them with an appropriate connective. The specific relationship between sentences will determine which connective will work best. Here are some common connectives for indicating specific types of relationships:

1. The second sentence gives an illustration or example: **first, for example, for instance, for one thing, to illustrate.**

2. The second sentence adds another point: **and, also, too, then, second, equally, for another thing, furthermore, moreover, in addition, similarly, next, again, above all, finally.**

3. The second sentence restates, summarizes, or shows a result: **in fact, so, thus, therefore, as a result, accordingly, in other words.**

4. The second sentence expresses a contrast: **but, still, yet, however, even so, by contrast, on the contrary, nevertheless, on the other hand.**

In the next passage, the connective **but** indicates the contrast between what many Americans believe about Niagara Falls and actual facts:

> Many Americans think that Niagara Falls is the highest waterfall in the world. **But,** Angel Falls in Venezuela, at 3,212 feet, is roughly twenty times higher.

The next paragraph contains a list of sentences following the topic sentence. The connectives **first, second, third,** and **finally** clearly indicate their relationship to one another, making them into a coherent passage. **For one thing, for another thing,** and **lastly** would have worked as well:

> Today, few old-growth forests still exist. But in patches here and there visitors can experience the exhilarating majesty of the ancient forests, forests populated with trees that range from 400 to 3,000 years of age. How can you get the most out of a visit to an old-growth forest? **First,** be quiet and walk slowly. **Second,** allow the atmosphere of the place to soak into your spirit. **Third,** let the trees speak to you. **Finally,** become a part of the forest community.

Connective Phrases and Clauses

When you revise a paragraph, you sometimes need more than a common connective to fill a gap between two sentences. You may need a longer phrase or clause or even a full sentence to fill in content between the parts. In the next paragraph, for instance, a clause beginning with a connective—**but when the rain does come**—sharpens the contrast and bridges the gap between the torrential downpours and the typical dry weather in certain arid regions of the world:

> Some arid regions of the world receive an average of only two- or three-hundredths of an inch of rain annually and may go for years without getting a drop. It usually comes in torrential downpours.

> Some arid regions of the world receive an average of only two- or three-hundredths of an inch of rain annually and may go for years

without getting a drop. **But when the rain does come,** it usually comes in torrential downpours.

❧ USING REFERENCES

Besides using connectives, you can link sentences with references to earlier words and phrases, by repeating words, by creating synonyms, and by using pronouns.

Word Repetition

The simplest way to use references for coherence within a paragraph is to repeat an important word or phrase. Repetition works especially well when it emphasizes the topic of the paragraph. The topic in the next paragraph, novelist Agatha Christie's mysterious disappearance, is established in the first two sentences by the words **mystery, mysterious,** and **disappearance.** But notice how the last sentence trails off because the writer doesn't pick up on those words:

> Agatha Christie earned world renown as the author of numerous **mystery** tales. But none of the fictional tales is more **mysterious** than the true story of her own **disappearance** in December of 1926. Waves of shock rumbled throughout the British public when the newspapers proclaimed that Christie had vanished. Not until several months later was she discovered, supposedly afflicted with amnesia, working as a nanny in a Yorkshire manor house. To this day, her fans are intrigued because she was gone for so long without being discovered.

In the next version, the writer revised the last sentence to repeat the words **mystery** and **disappearance:**

> Agatha Christie earned world renown as the author of numerous **mystery** tales. But none of the fictional tales is more **mysterious** than the true story of her own **disappearance** in December of 1926. Waves of shock rumbled throughout the British public when the newspapers proclaimed that Christie had vanished. Not until several months later was she discovered, supposedly afflicted with amnesia, working as a nanny in a Yorkshire manor house. To this day, her fans are intrigued by the **mystery** of her **disappearance.**

The repetition of key words links the last sentence to the first, establishing coherence and reinforcing the topic as well. Just as you can make a paragraph coherent by repeating key words or phrases, you can do the same for an entire paper when you link paragraphs by repeating key words or phrases.

Pronouns

A second kind of reference is through pronouns like **she, he, it, they, this, that, his, her, their, some,** or **another.** A pronoun is a word that gets its meaning by referring to an earlier word or phrase. In the next example, the pronouns **they** and **their** keep the focus of the paragraph on people born under the astrological sign Virgo:

> Virgos are simple and gentle people, with a need to serve humanity. Careful and precise by nature, **they** make excellent secretaries and nurses. **Their** warm, shining eyes and **their** bright appearances conceal **their** burning desire for love.

In the next passage, not only does the pronoun **he,** in reference to Ben Franklin, ensure coherence, but its repetition also links the series of sentences into a forceful pattern, with four sentences in a row beginning with **he:**

> In *Poor Richard's Almanack,* **Benjamin Franklin** advises colonial Americans against leisure activities, noting that "sloth" brings illness and shortens life. **He** claims that only labor is truly satisfying. **He** warns that to be in debt is to fear the day when repayment must be made. **He** also says that the more you spend, the more you want. If **he** were still around, this advocate of the spartan life would surely advise today's Americans to increase their eight-hour workday, stop their credit-card buying sprees, and break their addiction to computer games and cable television.

Synonyms

A third reference strategy is the use of synonyms. With synonyms, instead of repeating a word directly, you repeat it indirectly with a word or phrase that has the same or a similar meaning (or you refer to it with a pronoun, which is a kind of synonym itself). For example, in the Benjamin Franklin paragraph above, notice how the last sentence shifts from the pronoun **he** to the synonym **this advocate of the spartan life,** another way of describing Franklin.

In the next paragraph, the writer uses the synonyms **bikes, them, a way, biking,** and **pedaling** rather than repeat **bicycling** or **bicycles** in each sentence:

> **Bicycling** in America has grown at an explosive rate. **Bicycles** used to be sold to parents for their children. Now those same parents buy **bikes** for themselves as well. Executives ride **them** to work in order to stay out of traffic jams. Suburbanites have found **a way** to do their shopping without competing for a parking place at the mall. High school and college students find **biking** an economical alternative to cars and buses. And even Grandma and Grandpa enjoy **pedaling** for exercise.

Like repeated words and phrases, synonyms can drive home the meaning of a passage. Throughout the next paragraph, for example, the various synonyms for **endangered** not only link the sentences but also restate and reinforce the topic—that the red wolf is an endangered species:

> The red wolf is an **endangered** species. Its numbers have **declined perilously,** both because of willful **slaughter** subsidized by government bounties and because of the wolf's **susceptibility** to the **deadly destruction** of intestinal parasites. And now the species may face total **extinction** because of its ability to breed with a closely related but far more numerous cousin, the coyote. Thus, having survived the worst that humans and worms can do, the red wolf is now **endangered** by the **loss** of its own distinguishing genes.

Remember that you can overuse synonyms, as well as word repetition and pronouns, so you'll often want to mix strategies in your own writing. Notice that the paragraph on wolves not only includes several synonyms for **endangered** but also repeats the word in the final sentence. The writer brings the paragraph full circle, thus clinching the point.

Sometimes you can use a synonym in order to sum up or synthesize one or more of your preceding statements. In the following passage, **such migrations** serves as a synonym for the phrase **travel long distances:**

> Eels, whales, salmon, turtles, and birds—and even bees and butterflies—**travel long distances,** sometimes thousands of miles annually over unmarked terrain, to reach specific spawning grounds or to find food or living space. While **such migrations** have been observed and recorded since ancient times, science offers no clear explanation of how animals navigate.

The summarizing synonym **such migrations** establishes coherence by linking the second sentence to the first. Synonyms that sum up are commonly accompanied by words like **such, this, these,** and **of this sort.**

✍ ARRANGING SENTENCES INTO STRUCTURAL PATTERNS

As a third major strategy of coherence, you can arrange sentences into structural patterns; this arrangement usually includes placing parallel ideas into parallel structures or organizing old and new information into proper sequences. This strategy is the most sophisticated way to give your writing coherence; keep it in mind as you revise your drafts.

Look for the possibility of arranging sentences into structural patterns whenever you make parallel points. Let's suppose that after researching the topic you conclude that in the 1960s, pop music was shaped by radically different geographic and cultural influences. You might write a paragraph like this:

> The 1960s brought to American pop music a fusion of radically different geographic and cultural influences. The influence of religion and mysticism which came from the East made popular such instruments as the tabla and the sitar. A Caribbean influence was southern in origin, branching into such forms as reggae and calypso, with their steel drums and marimbas. But folk music, perhaps the most important influence on pop music at the time, with its simple melodies and melodramatic lyrics, came from the West, particularly from Britain and the American Midwest.

The paragraph has a clear topic sentence and contains interesting details, but it also has ideas that lend themselves to a parallel structural arrangement. Because the separate influences all "came from" somewhere—the East, the South, or the West—you could sharpen the relationship of the details to the topic sentence if you organized the paragraph according to geographic sources:

> The 1960s brought to American pop music a fusion of radically different geographic and cultural influences. **From the East** came the influence of religion and mysticism, which made popular such instruments as the tabla and the sitar. **From the South** came the Caribbean influence, branching into such forms as reggae and calypso, with their steel drums and marimbas. **And from the West,** particularly from Britain and the American Midwest, came folk music, with its simple melodies and melodramatic lyrics, resulting in perhaps the most important influence on pop music at the time.

If you read the paragraph aloud, you'll see that such patterning does more than sharpen relationships. It moves readers from sentence to sentence, guiding them on the journey from one idea to the next, the goal of coherence. Note that patterning does not mean mechanical repetition. The last phrase in this series does not repeat the pattern exactly. It begins with **and** and is separated from the verb **came** by the prepositional phrase **particularly from Britain and the American Midwest.** Repeating the words **from the . . . came** organizes the paragraph into a smooth flow of sentences. Breaking the pattern in the last sentence helps to add interest and variety. If you become pattern-conscious, you are in a better position both to recognize the lack of coherence in your first drafts and to revise them effectively.

Old and New Information

Readers expect a sentence in a sequence to start where the previous one left off. That is, a sentence generally begins with OLD INFORMATION, some reference to what has already been said. And then it moves to NEW INFOR-MATION, an idea that carries the thought further. So, you can create coherence by arranging information into the order a reader expects: first old information (in the subject) then new information (in the predicate). Read through the next paragraph to see what happens when you violate this principle:

> *Naked Came the Stranger* was probably the most interesting literary hoax of the twentieth century. Staff members of the newspaper *New York Newsday* wrote the chapters of the book independently, without knowledge of each other's work. It was intended as an incoherent pornographic novel, to be published under the pseudonym "Penelope Ashe."

What happens when you violate this principle about old and new information is that you create a moment of uncertainty for your readers. The first sentence presents *Naked Came the Stranger* as a literary hoax. Readers expect that the second sentence will begin with either a reference to the book or a reference to literary hoaxes. But the second sentence does neither; it opens with a new topic, **staff members of the newspaper *New York Newsday*.** If you arrange the second sentence so that it begins with old information, like **the chapters of the book,** you satisfy your readers' expectations. In this paragraph, that arrangement of old and new information also creates a structural pattern of coherence with ***Naked Came the Stranger* was . . . The chapters of the book were . . . It was . . . :**

> ***Naked Came the Stranger* was** probably the most interesting literary hoax of the twentieth century. **The chapters of the book were** written independently by staff members of the newspaper *New York Newsday*, without knowledge of each other's work. **It was** intended as an incoherent pornographic novel, to be published under the pseudonym "Penelope Ashe."

✍ CONNECTING PARAGRAPHS

To link one paragraph to another within your draft, you can use the same strategies that link sentences within a paragraph. Just remember that the indentation which marks a new paragraph makes readers experience a greater gap between paragraphs than they do between sentences within a single paragraph. So you have to pay special attention in order to smooth the transition from one paragraph to another.

For example, the second paragraph in the next passage lacks a strong enough bridge to connect it to the first paragraph:

> Capital punishment complicates the administration of justice. It leads to lengthy trials and unjustified verdicts, and it places a burden on courts

> of appeal. It also forces taxpayers to support all those waiting their turn for execution on death row.
>
> **Furthermore,** the Eighth Amendment to the Constitution bars "cruel and unusual" punishment, and execution is surely both cruel and unusual. There is simply no humane way to kill people. Nor are gas chambers, electric chairs, or lethal injections "usual" causes of death.

In this case, the connective **Furthermore** doesn't provide a strong enough link between paragraphs; the word implies that the second paragraph will simply add some new evidence to the argument against capital punishment. In fact, what the second paragraph does is introduce a much more complicated argument against capital punishment than the fact that it inconveniences courts and taxpayers. The second paragraph agrues that capital punishmnent denies Americans their constitutional right not to be punished in a cruel and unusual manner. Capital punishment kills—unusually as well as cruelly—it notes. To move the reader from the less significant to the weightier topic, a more elaborate transition would help, one that points out the difference beween the topics in the two paragraphs and that builds a stronger bridge between them as well:

> Capital punishment complicates the administration of justice. It leads to lengthy trials and unjustified verdicts, and it places a burden on courts of appeal. It also forces taxpayers to support all those waiting their turn for execution on death row.
>
> **But when a person's life is at stake, such inconveniences seem trivial. A far more fundamental objection to capital punishment is a constitutional one:** the Eighth Amendment to the Constitution bars "cruel and unusual" punishment, and execution is surely both cruel and unusual. There is simply no humane way to kill people. Nor are gas chambers, electric chairs, or lethal injections "usual" causes of death.

It took two sentences to bridge the gap here. The first notes how trivial the inconveniences mentioned in the earlier paragraph are; the second explicitly states that the topic of the new paragraph is **a far more fundamental objection.** The two-sentence transition carefully guides the reader across the large gap from one idea to the next.

✌ PLAYING WITH COHERENCE

Writing that employs synonyms, pronouns, and patterns to create coherence is considered sophisticated and well crafted. Writers who understand how to create coherence are considered thoughtful crafters of prose. So, especially when you're revising papers, look for opportunities to make your own writing more coherent.

EXERCISES

Using Connectives

Improve the coherence of each paragraph below, either by inserting a common connective between sentences that lack bridges between them, or by creating your own transitional phrase to bridge the gap. As an alternate assignment, revise a paragraph in a paper of your own to improve its coherence.

EXAMPLE

To ease the legal problems faced by couples involved in divorce, more than one-half the states have passed laws accepting simple incompatibility as legitimate grounds for dissolving a marriage. No-fault divorce is proving to have unexpected disadvantages. It may be doing as much harm as good.

↓

To ease the legal problems faced by couples involved in divorce, more than one-half the states have passed laws accepting simple incompatibility as legitimate grounds for dissolving a marriage. **Yet,** no-fault divorce is proving to have unexpected disadvantages. **In fact,** it may be doing as much harm as good.

OR

To ease the legal problems faced by couples involved in divorce, more than one-half the states have passed laws accepting simple incompatibility as legitimate grounds for dissolving a marriage. **Like some other well-meant reforms,** no-fault divorce is proving to have unexpected disadvantages. **In some situations,** it may be doing as much harm as good.

A. The necktie has many symbolic and psychological meanings. Worn with a full business suit, a tie can be a form of armor, a defense, and an assertion of power. The necktie is used as a signal to other men, announcing, "We all speak the same language."

B. The clang, clang, clang of the trolley could be heard in every major city of the nation before World War II. After the war, people moved to the suburbs and the government built superhighways; electrically powered vehicles were replaced by cars and buses. City planners are looking into the possibility of building new trolley systems, because they are cheaper and cleaner than other forms of mass transportation.

C. The debate over censorship in the media has shifted from television, film, and literature to the Internet. More and more states have passed laws to restrict the transmission of indecent information and images. Congress passed two telecommunications bills which contain provisions restricting pornography. These state and federal laws are supposed to protect minors from obscene materials. Opponents of such laws say they infringe upon First Amendment rights guaranteeing freedom of expression. The debate, like the Internet itself, is not going to go away quickly.

The Darker Side of Chocolate

Revise the following sentences into an explanatory essay about the history of chocolate and social consequences of chocolate production. Then, where necessary, improve the coherence between sentences and larger components by using the strategies of coherence discussed in this chapter.

1. Do you ever think about the history involved in producing that chocolate bar?

2. Do you ever think about the social conditions involved in producing that chocolate bar?

3. You enjoy the chocolate bar so much.

4. The Aztecs first made chocolate from the cocoa bean.

5. They mixed the crushed cocoa bean with spices and chili.

6. That made a drink called *xocoatl*.

7. *Xocoatl* meant bitter water.

8. They usually reserved xocoatl for the nobility.

9. Nonetheless, the Aztecs served the foamy brew to Cortez and his conquistadors.

10. These Spanish explorers brought the bitter bean back to Europe in 1519.

11. Europeans learned to grow it in their equatorial African colonies.

12. Europeans learned to grow it in their equatorial South American colonies.

13. Europeans learned to mix chocalate with sugar rather than spices.

14. It wasn't an instant success.

15. The French at first considered chocolate a barbarous product.

16. The French at first considered chocolate a noxious drink.

17. It caught on slowly.

18. By the mid-eighteenth century chocolate was as popular as coffee.

19. Chocolate remained exclusively a drink until the nineteenth century.

20. Then chemists learned to add cocoa butter back to the mix.

21. By adding cocoa butter, they produced solid chocolate.

22. Solid chocolate would melt in your mouth and your hand.

23. Chocolate bars became popular in World War I.

24. In World War I, armies provided it to their troops for both energy and morale.

25. Chocolate became the most popular candy of all time.

26. It became popular in the Western world.

27. In those African nations cocoa farming enslaves workers.

28. Cocoa farming forced them to work for pennies a day.

29. The African nations are former European colonies.

30. The African nations are like Ivory Coast.

31. The workers on a cocoa plantation are generally paid from $13 to $160 per year.

32. Think about that next time.

33. You bite into a scrumptious milk chocolate bar.

Using Reference

Improve the coherence of each paragraph below by using pronouns or synonyms for reference. Be sure to write out each paragraph. As an alternate assignment, revise a paragraph in a draft of your own to improve its coherence.

EXAMPLE

Dancing is a cultural universal. In many cultures, dancing helps define group identity and enhance morale. Dancing also has a central place in festive or religious events, and dancing may be an important factor in courtship.

↓

Dancing is a cultural universal. In many cultures, **it** helps define group identity and enhance morale. **It** also has a central place in festive or religious events, and **it** may be an important factor in courtship.

A. Chicago, at the southern tip of Lake Michigan, has spent a half century and billions of dollars developing a good water system. Chicago draws a billion gallons a day from the lake, to serve over 5 million people. But when Chicago's lake water became almost too dirty for treatment, Chicago was forced to consider getting water elsewhere—and paying more for it.

B. Patchwork quilts are among the antiques increasing steadily in worth. Once common in every household, the quilts were treasured, too, by the pioneers who made the quilts. The quilts provided color and gaiety for the crude, drab pioneer cabins. The quilts' combination of small, various-shaped pieces in geometric designs made use of otherwise useless scraps of fabric. And since many patchwork pieces were cut from old clothing, the quilts even provided a sense of continuity with the past.

C. An American company under government contract is often faced with the choice of buying American-made goods, which are expensive, or foreign-made goods, which are cheaper. If the American company buys American goods, the company may anger consumers by failing to keep prices low. But if the company buys foreign goods, the company may endanger the jobs of American workers. Confronting the issue, Congress passed a law compelling American companies with government contracts to give preference to American goods and services.

The Giant Panda

Revise the following sentences into a brief draft that explains how the giant panda may resemble a bear but is a closer relative of the raccoon. Then, where necessary, improve the coherence between sentences by using the strategies of coherence discussed in this chapter.

1. Have you ever seen the giant panda?

2. Then you know how closely it resembles a bear.

3. The shape of a panda resembles a bear's shape.

4. The panda has a massive body, a large head, and short, stubby legs.

5. The panda is built like a bear.

6. The panda can be as long as six feet and as heavy as 300 pounds.

7. The panda also resembles a bear because it can stand on its hind legs.

8. And also bearlike is the way it uses its sharp claws to climb trees.

9. Bears walk on the soles of their feet.

10. The panda also walks on the soles of its feet.

11. The panda has a distinctive "harlequin" outfit.

12. It has a basically creamy white body with black bursts on the ears.

13. It has black bursts over the eyes.

14. It has black bursts around the chest and back.

15. It has black bursts down the forelegs and along the hind legs.

16. The harlequin outfit is the only trademark.

17. The trademark recalls the panda's true relative.

18. The panda's true relative is the raccoon.

Using Structural Patterns

Improve the coherence of each paragraph below by arranging sentences into structural patterns or by ordering old and new information. Be sure to write out each paragraph. As an alternate assignment, revise a paragraph in a draft of your own to improve its coherence.

EXAMPLE

To become finalists in the competition for scholarships, the semifinalists must supply biographical information, maintain high academic standing, and perform well on a second examination. In addition, their high school principal must endorse them.

To become finalists in the competition for scholarships, the semifinalists must supply biographical information, maintain high academic standing, and perform well on a second examination. In addition, **they must earn the endorsement of their high school principal.**

A. For Northerners, Lincoln was a hero because he ended slavery and saved the Union. But because he destroyed one of the staples of their economy, Lincoln was regarded as a villain by Southerners.

B. Because they are produced when conscious controls are lowered, doodles reveal personality in much the same way dreams do. Psychologists at Michigan State University found that students who draw houses on their class notes yearn for security, while aggressive personalities draw sharp objects. Spiders, bugs, and mice are drawn by deeply troubled people. And if you have a "normal" personality, you are likely to draw pictures of domestic animals—dogs, cats, and horses.

C. The weather forecaster on the evening news may have all the latest information from radar and satellites to give an accurate forecast. Old-timers claim you can be just as accurate by watching natural signs. For an indication of fair skies ahead, look for gnats swarming in the setting sun. Noisy woodpeckers signal rain on the way. When bubbles collect in the middle of your morning coffee, fair weather is coming. But it's time to look for an umbrella when the bubbles ring around the edge.

Gene Blues

Read the following twenty-one sentences to get a sense of their meaning. Then, by (1) reordering Sections A–D and (2) rearranging the sentences within each section, construct a coherent essay that explains why the creation of new forms of life through gene transplants is frightening.

A.
1. Because transplanted genes can be inserted into bacteria which are able to reproduce themselves in succeeding generations, the result of the transplant is a permanent new life form.

2. No one knows precisely how it may react to the environment outside the laboratory or to humans and animals.

3. These creations are a part of recombinant DNA research, which involves transplanting one or more foreign genes into loops of DNA in a bacteria.

4. Its observable physical characteristics are all that is known about this new life.

B.
1. Perhaps scientists, who usually oppose public control of their research, have agreed too readily to those guidelines because they, too, will feel the consequences of a mistake.

2. But so little is known about the newly created organisms that scientists don't know whether the safeguards are adequate.

3. And the safeguards do not apply to commercial companies like Eli Lilly and General Electric, which are also conducting research in this field.

4. In response to these fears, the National Institutes of Health have offered a set of guidelines to ensure the safety of recombinant DNA research.

5. They cannot know whether the safeguards are sufficient.

6. One safeguard is a complete ban on altering human sperm and ova.

7. No such mistakes have been made yet, though perhaps one is one too many.

8. Another safeguard requires that only weakened *Escherichia coli* bacteria be used, so that they will not survive for long away from the lab.

C. 1. Perhaps these creations will wreck the environment, eating up chemicals or destroying the soil.

2. Some people are afraid that cancer viruses transplanted into bacteria will spread cancer.

3. And since most of the experiments use the bacteria *E. coli*, which live in humans, a new combination may turn out to be highly infectious to humans.

4. They are afraid that a transplant between two completely different species, such as frogs and bacteria, will create new diseases to which humans will be susceptible.

5. Because of this uncertainty, fears have flared up.

D. 1. No one knows what would happen if some of these organisms were to escape from the laboratory, but doubtless there is a risk of disease or death in humans.

2. Scientists are creating new forms of life, and these new creatures do not have bolts through their necks, like Frankenstein monsters.

3. These forms of life involve gene transplants and are locked away in research laboratories, hopefully in safekeeping.

4. Yet they may be more dangerous than any Frankenstein monster could ever be.

11

Rearrangement and Repetition for Emphasis

Preview

This lesson focuses on how to use rearrangement and repetition in order to make a piece of writing compelling and forceful as well as appealing. Writers emphasize words and phrases by moving them to the beginnings or endings of sentences or by using them to interrupt normal sentence order. The same is true of sentences within paragraphs. Using rearrangement patterns like the INTRODUCTORY IT, the INTRODUCTORY WHAT, or the PASSIVE can create emphasis. Besides taking advantage of emphatic positions and standard patterns, ideas can be highlighted through repetition and balance.

✌ EMPHASIS

Skilled speakers use a variety of techniques both to keep an audience interested and to emphasize their main ideas. They change rhythms, speak louder or softer, pound the podium, or stand motionless. They repeat key phrases and sentences. But writers can't pound on the lectern, turn up the volume, or stand still. What they can do is rearrange words and phrases and repeat structures in order to emphasize ideas as well as make their writing appealing and forceful.

✌ REARRANGING

When you REARRANGE a sentence for emphasis, you need to remember two important facts about word order in English:

- The beginning and ending positions in a sentence play different roles. The end of the sentence is the most emphatic position; this is where writers usually place the most important word or phrase. The beginning, the second most emphatic position, usually tells readers what the

159

sentence is about and in some way connects the sentence to what has been said before, in order to ensure coherence.

■ English word order is relatively fixed, with most sentences following a subject-verb-object (or complement) pattern. When writers depart from this usual pattern, they change the meaning or emphasis within a sentence and can even affect how an individual sentence relates to other sentences within a paragraph.

❧ TAKING ADVANTAGE OF BEGINNINGS AND ENDINGS

In the sentence below, the title of the tourist guide, "Who's Whoooooo," occurs in the middle, where it receives little attention:

> The U.S. Travel Service offers tourists **"Who's Whoooooo,"** a guide to haunted houses.

If you wish to emphasize the title of the guide, simply shift that phrase to the beginning or end of the sentence:

> **"Who's Whoooooo"** is a guide to haunted houses that the U.S. Travel Service offers tourists.

OR

> The U.S. Travel Service offers tourists a guide to haunted houses— **"Who's Whoooooo."**

What's true of the order of words within sentences is also true of sentence positions within paragraphs. You can guide the reader's attention to your major points by placing the most important sentences at either the beginning or the ending of the paragraph. For example, the opening and closing sentences in the next paragraph emphasize that skateboarding is dangerous:

> **Skateboarding may be the most exhilarating of all sports, but it's also the most dangerous.** Apparently, the thrill comes from the speed— some champs do sixty-five miles per hour—and from the challenge posed by the unlimited possibilities for new stunts. So many daredevils have tried stunts like "pipe riding" or the "gorilla grip," that in one recent year skateboarders suffered over 130,000 injuries—20 of them fatal. Enthusiasts insist that what you do with skateboards has no limit. **At least 20 of them learned otherwise.**

The danger of skateboarding is emphasized by the short, crisp closing sentence. The final word—**otherwise**—acknowledges that death does set limits on skateboarding. The paragraph below contains the same information but rearranges the sentences to emphasize that the dangers of skateboarding are less important than its exhilaration. Notice particularly the first and last sentences:

> **Although it may be the most dangerous sport, skateboarding is also the most exhilarating.** Injuries do occur—over 130,000 in one recent year, 20 of them fatal. **But** consider the thrill that comes from the speed—some champs do sixty-five miles per hour—and from the challenge posed by the unlimited possibilities for new stunts, like "pipe riding" and the "gorilla grip." **While some practitioners may inevitably perish in trying new tricks, enthusiasts insist that what skateboards can do has no limit.**

The first sentence signals the paragraph's emphasis—the fact that skateboarding is **exhilarating.** Although the second sentence acknowledges that injuries may occur, the connective **But** at the start of the third sentence suggests that the thrills of skateboarding outweigh its dangers. Finally, the key statement **what skateboards can do has no limit** occupies the paragraph's most emphatic position—its end. When you control emphasis, you control meaning in sentences or paragraphs.

ಌ USING REARRANGEMENT PATTERNS

Certain rearrangement patterns can help you emphasize your ideas. The first of these is the INTRODUCTORY WHAT pattern. To make the pattern, you insert **what** and a form of **be**—either **is, was, are,** or **were**—into a sentence along with rearranging some words. The introductory what pattern highlights the contrast between two sentences:

> After the last bunch of guys left the party, the house seemed unnaturally quiet. The argument when our parents came home was not so quiet.

> After the last bunch of guys left the party, the house seemed unnaturally quiet. **What** was not so quiet **was** the argument when our parents came home.

Like the pattern with **what,** the INTRODUCTORY IT pattern, which inserts **it** and a form of **be,** along with **who** or **that,** also highlights contrasts. Writing about a mayor who had received more applause than the president, you might say:

> The president was applauded enthusiastically. But the mayor of New York City received the largest ovation.

But by revising the second sentence into the introductory it pattern, you can suggest an even stronger contrast between the two ovations:

> The president was applauded enthusiastically. But **it was** the mayor of New York City who received the largest ovation.

The PASSIVE is the most commonly used and probably the most commonly abused rearrangement pattern. To construct a passive from an active sentence, move the object noun to the front, add a form of **be,** and move the subject noun into a phrase with **by.** When you place the subject noun in a **by phrase,** you emphasize its agency—its role in carrying out the action of the verb:

> The Food and Drug Administration (FDA) inspects meat for contamination.

> Meat **is inspected** for contamination **by the FDA.**

Because it shifts the object noun phrase to the front of the sentence, the passive can help you control the flow of sentences in a paragraph as well as emphasize the agent in a sentence. Remember that the first part of a sentence usually contains information linked to earlier sentences. The second sentence in the next example should have **the blast** in the initial position to link it with the subject of the first sentence, **a nasty explosion:**

> A nasty explosion rocked Lab B in the Science Building yesterday. A canister of benzene caused the blast.

You can correct the problem by revising the second sentence into a passive:

> A nasty explosion rocked Lab B in the Science Building yesterday. **The blast was caused by a canister of benzene.**

You can sometimes omit the **by phrase** of a passive—especially when the **by phrase** contains information repeated elsewhere in your draft or commonly known by your readers. For instance, if your readers know that most people call Einstein the twentieth century's greatest mind, you can eliminate the phrase **by most people** and save three words, as in the next example:

> Most people call Einstein the twentieth century's greatest mind.

> Einstein is called the twentieth century's greatest mind **by most people.**

OR

Einstein is called the twentieth century's greatest mind.

While omitting the **by phrase** can help you tighten your sentences, it can also lead to a common, and sometimes unethical, misuse of the passive—to hide responsibility. In the next example, the memo writer does not want to admit that her office is firing ten employees, so she phrases the act in the passive and conceals who is responsible for the actions:

> As of July 30, ten members of the design staff will be terminated **by the personnel office**.

$$\downarrow$$

> As of July 30, ten members of the design staff will be terminated.

Readers often feel cheated or manipulated when writers do not reveal the agent of an action. So be careful not to omit the **by phrase** unless your readers already know the information in it or unless leaving it out will not in any way "cheat" your readers.

❧ BREAKING ESTABLISHED PATTERNS

As you write, you establish patterns that your readers come to expect. If you occasionally break these patterns, you can create emphasis in paragraphs and sentences. For example, following several long sentences, you can provide a striking and compelling contrast by writing a short sentence or even a deliberate fragment:

> Legend has it that Robin Hood was a noble criminal leading a band of "Merry Men" who robbed from the rich and gave to the poor—loyal servants of King Richard, unfairly pursued by the evil Sheriff of Nottingham. The historical Robin was a small-time mugger leading a band of crooks and drunks who robbed, raped, and swindled rich and poor alike. **So much for legends!**

You can achieve emphasis not only by disrupting your own writing patterns but also by departing from the basic sentence patterns of the language. In English, the subject-verb-object pattern is so common that readers tend to notice any departure from it. You can create emphasis either by changing the order of the words or by interrupting the normal movement of the sentence. One uncommon but dynamic option places a critical word or phrase at the beginning of a sentence. Notice how, by moving **Barcelona** to the front of the next example, you can make that word nearly shout at the reader:

The very word *Barcelona* evokes images of a vibrant, tumultuous, exotic city.

Barcelona—the very word evokes images of a vibrant, tumultuous, exotic city.

The word you've moved to the front of the sentence may be set off with a dash—as above—or with punctuation marks like ellipses, exclamation points, and colons. Sometimes you can begin with a verb, along with an adverb like **only** or **first,** or a negative like **nowhere, not until,** or **never:**

The governor came first, then her economic advisers.

First came the governor, then her economic advisers.

When you interrupt a sentence with a word, phrase, or clause, you emphasize the interrupting element and what immediately follows it:

Amnesty International—**more than 200,000 members strong**—uses the force of public opinion to combat the violation of human rights worldwide.

Interrupting one sentence with another sentence can be especially striking:

Most ethnic cuisines include a flat bread such as pita, lahvosh, tortillas, chapatis, focaccia, and matzoh. North African, Armenian, Mexican, Indian, Italian, and Jewish are a few of these cuisines.

Most ethnic cuisines—**North African, Armenian, Mexican, Indian, Italian, and Jewish are a few**—include a flat bread such as pita, lahvosh, tortillas, chapati, focaccia, and matzoh.

Rearrangement will work best if you don't overdo it. Rearrange sentence parts only when you need to create emphasis or control the movement from one sentence to another.

ᔐ REPETITION

Advertisers deliberately repeat words and phrases in order to drive home a message to potential customers. Using such REPETITION, Mitsubishi Motors described its Galant as "**Here** today. **Here** tomorrow." Kodak asserted that "Kodak Gold makes any **light** the right **light.**" Terminix proclaimed its exterminating prowess when it announced "Nobody **bugs bugs** like Terminix." Sometimes the words and phrases are not repeated exactly but only balanced to correspond in rhythm and structure. So Secret Anti-Perspirant & Deodorant told customers that "it's strong enough **for a man,** but made **for a woman,**" and Naya bottled water's motto was "**Hungry** for **life. Thirsty** for **Naya.**" The strategies of repetition that work in advertising copy can work just as well in your writing. They can help you achieve emphasis and produce pleasing, dynamic drafts.

You can use repetition to emphasize key terms in sentences. The next sentence matter-of-factly states Grandfather's condition before he died:

> My grandfather had nothing left except memories before he died.

Repeating the word **nothing** makes Grandfather's condition much more poignant:

> My grandfather had **nothing** left before he died, **nothing** except memories.

Repetition can emphasize, and it can direct the reader's attention to important contrasts. In the next sentence, you can strengthen the contrast between Sally's loafing **in the sun** and her friends' working **on the job** by repeating **spent long hot days:**

> While all Sally's friends spent **long hot days on the job,** she **spent long hot days in the sun,** soaking up a tan.

Sometimes you can omit words and phrases in repeated constructions in order to produce more concise and more forceful statements:

> Some lawyers are arrogant, ~~and~~ some ~~lawyers are~~ simply reserved.

> **Some lawyers are arrogant, some simply reserved.**

When you revise, look for places where you can use repetition and balance to achieve emphasis or to reinforce a contrast. You can make the following two sentences into a far stronger and more concise single sentence by changing **other students drink beer** into **for others** in order to contrast that phrase with **for some students:**

> Beer drinking has become a way of life for some students. And other students drink beer in order to escape.

> Beer drinking has become a way of life **for some students** and a means of escape **for others.**

In the next pair of sentences, the writer seized the opportunity to produce a contrasting pair of infinitive phrases that reinforce her point:

> ~~Do you~~ believe that children are immune to constantly repeated violence? ~~If you do, you are~~ ignoring the most basic principles of developmental psychology.

$$\downarrow$$

> **To believe** that children are immune to constantly repeated violence is **to ignore** the most basic principles of developmental psychology.

✌ PLAYING WITH REARRANGEMENT AND REPETITION

The exercises provide opportunities to play with rearrangement and repetition structures, constructing them, moving them around, and using them to write economically and to focus your sentences and paragraphs. When you're drafting or revising papers of your own, remember to look for opportunities to use rearrangement and repetition because such strategies can help you create compelling prose that emphasizes your ideas in subtle and powerful ways.

EXERCISES

Rearrangement and Repetition Within Sentences I

You can make a word or phrase in each of the sentences below more emphatic if you rearrange the parts to take advantage of sentence positions or repetition. Revise the sentences as indicated by the parenthetical suggestions.

EXAMPLE

International economics since World War II has become too complex for any single theory to explain or for any single government to control. [Emphasize the phrase "since World War II" by rearranging phrases.]

Since World War II, international economics has become too complex for any single theory to explain or for any single government to control.

OR

International economics has become—**since World War II**—too complex for any single theory to explain or for any single government to control.

A. Gourmet cooks and health food nuts ignore Shakespeare's warning that onions and garlic destroy "sweet breath." [Emphasize the agency of "gourmet cooks and health food nuts" with a passive sentence.]

B. Alfred Nobel hoped to be remembered for his peace prize, not his invention of dynamite. [Emphasize Nobel's hope with an introductory what pattern.]

C. Alan Shepard, Jr., was the first American in space, and he also was the one to hit a golf ball on the moon for the first time. [With a balanced structure, emphasize the contrast between hitting a golf ball and being the first in space.]

D. The gondolas of hot-air racing balloons are equipped with controls to change the altitude and direction of the craft, but not the speed. Accuracy counts in balloon racing; speed does not count. [Emphasize that accuracy matters more than speed in balloon racing with an introductory it pattern in the second sentence.]

167

E. Teddy Roosevelt miraculously survived being shot in the chest when he was running for president in 1912, the bullet striking his wadded-up campaign speech and his metal eyeglass case. [By interrupting the sentence with the final phrase, emphasize how miraculous Roosevelt's survival was.]

Marilyn

Using rearrangement wherever appropriate, revise the sentences below into a finished draft that explains why Marilyn Monroe was a tragic figure who still fascinates the public. Not every sentence can be rearranged; you'll be able to make some sentences into structures you've studied in other chapters.

1. The name *Marilyn* still evokes magic for moviegoers.

2. Marilyn Monroe has lost none of her power to move us.

3. Marilyn Monroe has lost none of her power to intrigue us.

4. Marilyn Monroe has lost none of her power to disturb us.

5. She does this more than thirty years after her death.

6. Her biography might have been written by Dickens.

7. As a child, she was abandoned by her parents.

8. And she grew up in an orphanage and foster care.

9. She was innocent, yet she was seductive.

10. She rose to meteoric success as an actress.

11. She became the symbol of the blond movie goddess of the 1950s.

12. But fame and fortune never made her happy.

13. She wanted to be known for her talent and intelligence.

14. She did not want to be known for her body.

15. She went through two famous and disastrous marriages.

16. One was with ballplayer Joe DiMaggio.

17. One was with playwright Arthur Miller.

18. And she supposedly had a romance with John F. Kennedy.

19. And she supposedly had a romance with Robert Kennedy.

20. She died in her apartment.

21. Apparently, she was a suicide.

22. Some fans and friends still claim [this].

23. She was killed by the CIA in order to erase her connections to the Kennedys.

Rearrangement and Repetition Within Sentences II

You can make a word or phrase in each of the sentences below more emphatic if you rearrange the parts to take advantage of sentence positions or repetition. Revise the sentences as indicated by the parenthetical suggestions.

EXAMPLE

Unlike baseball, football is a ruthless, warlike game, according to comedian George Carlin. [By rearrangement, emphasize that football is "a ruthless, warlike game."]

Unlike baseball, according to comedian George Carlin, **football is a ruthless, warlike game.**

A. Martha's Vineyard is blessed with more than its share of good restaurants, and it is blessed with less than its share of street crime. [Emphasize the contrast between "good restaurants" and "street crime" with a balanced construction.]

B. The country that used to be called Ceylon is now named Sri Lanka, which means "resplendent land" in Sinhalese. [Highlight "Sri Lanka" by shifting that phrase to the front of the sentence.]

C. In 1922, the relentless Howard Carter became the first human being to enter King Tut's royal tomb in more than 3,000 years. He had been digging in the Egyptian Valley of the Kings for more than six years. [Interrupt the first sentence with the second in order to show how "relentless" Howard Carter was.]

D. "Biopiracy," the plundering of the Amazon's medicinal plants by pharmaceutical companies, is considered a major threat to Brazil's economy by the Brazilian government. The Brazilian government introduced legislation to regulate "bioprospecting" in an effort to bolster the nation's economic prospects. [By making the second sentence passive, to balance the first sentence, emphasize the actions taken by the Brazilian government.]

E. First-year psychology students were given a choice between writing a term paper and participating in experiments that involved electric-shock machines. That was some choice they were given. [Highlight the dilemma of the students' "choice" by making the last sentence an emphatic fragment.]

Angel Island: A Story Worth Preserving

Rearrange sentences and paragraphs, whenever appropriate, in order to emphasize that the tragic history of Angel Island needs to be preserved to honor the memory of those who were unfairly persecuted there. Not every sentence can be rearranged; you'll be able to revise some sentences into structures you've studied in other chapters.

1. San Francisco's Angel Island is like New York's Ellis Island.
2. It was used to process immigrants before they could enter America.

3. It is unlike New York's Ellis Island.
4. Ellis Island is well known as the first stop on these shores for European immigrants.

5. Angel Island is less well known as the final stop for Chinese immigrants trying to enter the United States.
6. Angel Island was opened in 1910.
7. It was meant to enforce the Chinese Exclusion Act of 1882.

8. The Exclusion Act was designed to keep Chinese immigrants from entering the country.
9. The Exclusion Act was designed to keep Chinese immigrants from taking jobs from European immigrants.

10. So Angel Island became a prison.
11. It kept would-be Chinese immigrants in cramped quarters.
12. It isolated them from their families.
13. And it kept them incarcerated for as long as twenty-two months.

14. Angel Island succeeded stunningly.

15. It closed because of a fire in 1940.

16. Before that, Angel Island had detained over 125,000 would-be Chinese immigrants.

17. And it kept them from entering the United States.

18. The Chinese population of California dropped from 9 percent to 1 percent.

19. This happened during Angel Island's lifetime.

20. And officials kept the story hush-hush.

21. The island's shameful history was preserved only in [this].

22. Poems, stories, and art were carved on its walls by prisoners.

23. Even that record would have been lost a few years ago.

24. At that time, the facilities were to be demolished.

25. But the Asian American community convinced California authorities to preserve the art and writing.

26. The government that [did this] also [did this].

27. It unfairly excluded the Chinese.

28. It opened its gates to their stories.

29. The opening of the gates creates a final, strange twist in the story of Angel Island.

Revising Sentences for Emphasis and Focus

In each of the following paragraphs, rearrange the sentence in brackets in order to emphasize an important point, to sharpen paragraph focus, or to establish sentence flow.

EXAMPLE

At the beginning of the twentieth century, the United States yearned to be a global power. In those days being a global power meant having a large navy. But the U.S. Navy was divided into two fleets, one on the East Coast, one on the West. [The completion of the Panama Canal allowed the nation to fulfill its dream.] By linking the two oceans, the canal made the separate fleets into one great navy.

↓

At the beginning of the twentieth century, the United States yearned to be a global power. In those days being a global power meant having a large navy. But the U.S. Navy was divided into two fleets, one on the East Coast, one on the West. **It was** the completion of the Panama Canal **that** allowed the nation to fulfill its dream. By linking the two oceans, the canal made the separate fleets into one great navy.

A. [Even the word *hiccup* is funny.] It imitates the silly sound you make when air bounces up and down inside you as if it's on a trampoline. But hiccups are funniest when someone else has them—right?

B. Elias Howe is given credit for inventing the sewing machine. [But Isaac Singer made it the most popular machine in history.] With his partner, Edward Clark, Singer developed the marketing techniques of installment buying and trade-ins. He also overcame the nineteenth-century prejudice that allowing women to operate machines violated the laws of nature.

C. Owls are known for their great wisdom. [But an owl should be known for its eyesight and hearing instead.] An owl's eyes are 100 times more sensitive to light than a human's and its ears can hear a mouse squeak from a half-mile away. So much of an owl's skull is filled by the organs it needs for its astonishing vision and hearing that there isn't much room for a large brain. As birds go, they aren't really all that intelligent.

Words and Things

Using rearrangement wherever appropriate, revise the sentences below into a draft that explains how words may originate. Not every sentence can be rearranged; you'll be able to make some sentences into structures you've studied in other chapters.

1. A language is like a biological system.

2. Its various parts are constantly adapting to new situations.

3. Words are the part of the system to study.

4. Words are the most interesting part.

5. Words are the cells of language.

6. They are forming.

7. They are dying.

8. They are splitting up into parts.

9. Words originate in all sorts of ways.

10. Some seem to have been made up purely for the way they sound.

11. Some words were originally the names of people or even towns.

12. These are like *sandwich* and *hamburger.*

13. The Earl of Sandwich didn't like to interrupt his gambling with meals.

14. So he had his servants slap some meat between two slices of bread.

15. It was a handy snack at the gaming table.

16. Thus the earl became immortal.

17. He gave his name to our favorite food.

18. *Hamburger* took its name from the city that originally made it famous.

19. The city was Hamburg, Germany.

20. The hamburger is the world's most famous sandwich.

21. It is never called a sandwich anymore.

22. The *burger* part of the word now means any kind of meat in a bun.

23. So we are inundated with various kinds of burgers.

24. We are inundated with *venisonburgers.*

25. We are inundated with *steakburgers.*

26. We are inundated with *doubleburgers.*

27. We are inundated with *cheeseburgers.*

28. And we are even inundated with *pizzaburgers.*

29. As long as the language is alive, its cells will continue to change.

30. The cells of the language are its words.

31. The cells will form.

32. The cells will die.

33. The cells will break up into parts to start the process again.

12

Tone

Preview

In this lesson, you'll learn about tone, the aspect of writing which readers can hear as they read. Writers must select words, structure sentences, and choose details to make their tone consistent with their purpose, their readers' expectations, and their own attitudes toward their subject matter. To write well you must learn to control tone. In the series of sentences about herbal remedies and paragraphs about asteroids passing near earth, you'll see how you can use word choice, sentence patterns, and details to change the tone of your writing.

❧ TONE AND THE WRITER'S VOICE

Let's suppose you witnessed some students cheating during an exam. Afterward, you write a letter to your best friend, who attends school in a different state. Your letter begins, "These jerks are going to ruin the curve, and my grade will go right into the john. They had crib sheets up their sleeves, if you can believe that stupidity." Then your professor calls you and asks you to write her a report about what you saw. Your report begins, "During the final examination on December 11, I observed two students apparently consulting handwritten notes concealed in their shirtsleeves."

Your tone in each of these pieces is different because both your purpose and your audience are different. TONE is the distinctive way that you express your feelings toward your subject according to what you hope to accomplish and how you relate to your audience. When we describe the tone of a piece of writing, we tend to use words that describe the way it sounds to us: angry, humorous, ironic, formal, negative, fair. We could say that tone is the way in which writers express their voice on paper.

In the letter to your friend, your tone is informal and angry. With such a familiar audience, you're comfortable using slang and letting your emotions out. You're probably interested in making your friend understand your anger and in evoking sympathy for your situation. In your report to the professor, however, your tone is more formal, since you don't know the professor very

174

well, and you recognize that she is a powerful person. Your objective is to provide her with the information she has requested, so you control the anger, provide concrete details, and choose longer words. The two situations are different, and so is your tone in each.

❧ TONE IN SENTENCES

Effective writers carefully select words, structure sentences, and choose details to build a consistent tone that fits the purpose of their writing. Suppose, for example, you are writing a paragraph or a brief essay on the increased sales of herbal remedies such as St. John's wort, echinacea, and ginkgo biloba. In your opening sentence, you include these two facts:

> Sales of herbal remedies such as St. John's wort, echinacea, and ginkgo biloba have doubled in the past decade.
>
> The increase in sales has been helped by statements from television advertisers, health-food advocates, and doctors.

You might put these facts together into a sentence like this:

> The sales of herbal remedies such as St. John's wort, echinacea, and ginkgo biloba, thanks to statements from television advertisers, health-food advocates, and doctors, have doubled in the past ten years.

This sentence sounds impartial and doesn't reveal your attitude toward the increased sales of herbal remedies. If you began with such a sentence, your reader would not know, at least at first, whether you thought the American public was wise or foolish in doubling its consumption of herbs such as St. John's wort. Of course, there's nothing wrong with sounding impartial. If your purpose is simply to inform your readers, it might be appropriate to write an impartial-sounding sentence. Journalists normally aim for such an impartial tone.

❧ CONTROLLING TONE

But let's suppose you've decided to write an essay for your health class critical of the American public's gullibility in flocking to "miracle cures." Because it sounds neutral, the sentence above wouldn't help you achieve that objective. If you know your purpose (to criticize certain behavior) and know who your readers will be (members of your health class), you can probably find the tone you need in a piece of writing; you can adjust your tone in the sentence to make it negative:

> The sales of herbal remedies such as St. John's wort, echinacea, and ginkgo biloba, thanks to the claims of Hollywood celebrities **hawking their "lifestyles of the rich and famous,"** health-food advocates **promoting "miracle" cures,** and doctors **pushing "alternative" treatments,** have doubled in the past ten years.

Hawking their "lifestyles of the rich and famous," promoting "miracle" cures, and **pushing "alternative" treatments** make herbal-remedy proponents seem overly aggressive. The phrases imply you are critical of the sales message. You can, of course, make the criticism more openly unfavorable. In the next example, the phrases **deceptions and lies, television snake-oil salesmen, health-food advocates,** and **medical quacks** let your readers know exactly where you stand and give your sentence a harsh negative tone:

> The sales of herbal remedies such as St. John's wort, echinacea, and ginkgo biloba, thanks to the **deceptions and lies of television snake-oil salesmen, health-food cranks, and medical quacks,** have doubled in the past ten years.

The harsh tone in the sentence would be especially appropriate for readers who share your negative attitudes toward herbal remedies. But for readers who don't start out on your side—and perhaps for some in your health class—the sentence may sound too strong and too opinionated. If so, you might try to suggest your feelings instead of stating them harshly. You can create a strongly negative tone without sounding as harsh by changing the diction:

> The sales of herbal remedies such as St. John's wort, echinacea, and ginkgo biloba, thanks to the claims of **some slick infomercial promoters, a few health-food cranks, and a handful of well-meaning chiropractors,** have doubled in the past ten years.

Let's suppose, however, that the more you research this topic, the more convinced you become that these herbal remedies deserve their wondrous reputation, leading you to change your mind about the purpose of the essay. So you now wish to praise the use of St. John's wort and the other herbs. With such changes in your attitude and purpose for writing, your tone will certainly change as well.

By choosing words and details with more positive associations, you can rewrite the sentence about increased herbal remedy sales to sound very different:

> The sales of herbal remedies such as St. John's wort, echinacea, and ginkgo biloba, thanks to **statements** from **celebrity television advertisers,** health-food **experts,** and **doctors,** have doubled in the past ten years.

OR

The sales of herbal remedies such as St. John's wort, echinacea, and ginkgo biloba, thanks to **reports** from **celebrity television advertisers,** health-food **experts,** and **doctors,** have doubled in the past ten years.

OR

The sales of herbal remedies such as St. John's wort, echinacea, and ginkgo biloba, thanks to the **testimony** of **celebrity television advertisers,** health-food **experts,** and **doctors,** have doubled in the past ten years.

Because **experts** seem more trustworthy than simple advocates, and because both **reports** and **testimony** carry more weight than mere **statements,** the three sentences above have a more positive tone than the original, more neutral version. But you can go even further in creating an approving tone by making the doctors who support herbal remedies seem more prestigious:

The sales of herbal remedies such as St. John's wort, echinacea, and ginkgo biloba, **helped by the testimony of** celebrity television advertisers, health-food experts, and **leading medical researchers,** have doubled in the past ten years.

This is an even more powerful endorsement of herbal remedies because **medical researchers** sound as if they are more knowledgeable and important than **doctors.**

✌ SENTENCE STRUCTURE

So far in every example the basic sentence structure has been the same ("The sales of herbal remedies . . . have doubled in the past ten years"), and you have changed the tone by replacing some important words. But you can also control tone by changing the structure of your sentences, by moving important ideas to more prominent positions. Let's take one more look at the bluntly worded sentence above:

The sales of herbal remedies such as St. John's wort, echinacea, and ginkgo biloba, thanks to the **deceptions and lies of television snake-oil salesmen, health-food cranks,** and **medical quacks,** have doubled in the past ten years.

You can make the tone seem more negative by moving the phrase about the deceptive behavior of health-food cranks and medical quacks to the end of the sentence, where it becomes more emphatic:

> In the past ten years, the sales of herbal remedies such as St. John's wort, echinacea, and ginkgo biloba have doubled, thanks to **the deceptions and lies of television snake-oil salesmen, health-food cranks, and medical quacks.**

Or you can also emphasize the deceptive behavior of health-food cranks by placing the phrase at the beginning of the sentence and setting it off with a dash to call more attention to the deception and lies:

> **The deceptions and lies of television snake-oil salesmen, health-food cranks, and medical quacks**—that's what has helped double the sales of herbal remedies such as St. John's wort, echinacea, and ginkgo biloba.

Emphasizing the phrase by moving it to either the beginning or the end position makes the sentence sound angrier.

❧ CLOSING THE DISTANCE BETWEEN THE WRITER AND READERS

The tone in the previous sentences about herbal remedies may range from negative to positive, but each sentence keeps a distance from the audience. Sometimes the writing situation calls for closing the distance between the writer and readers, making it more personal. To close the distance, you have a number of options. The simplest is to introduce yourself into the sentence as **I**:

> I find it hard to believe, but the sales of herbal remedies such as St. John's wort, echinacea, and ginkgo biloba, spurred on by the claims of television snake-oil salesmen, health-food cranks, and medical quacks, have doubled in the past ten years.

You can also close the gap if you establish a relationship between yourself and the reader by asking a question:

> **Why have the sales of herbal remedies such as St. John's wort, echinacea, and ginkgo biloba doubled in the past ten years?** Largely because of the claims of television snake-oil salesmen, health-food cranks, and medical quacks.

> OR

> **Who is responsible for the skyrocketing sales of herbal remedies such as St. John's wort, echinacea, and ginkgo biloba?** Mainly television snake-oil salesmen, health-food cranks, and medical quacks.

An even more direct way of relating to readers is by addressing them as **you**:

You may be surprised to learn that over the past ten years the sales of herbal remedies such as St. John's wort, echinacea, and ginkgo biloba have doubled, in large part because of the claims of television snake-oil salesmen, health-food cranks, and medical quacks.

OR

Did **you** know that, thanks to the claims of television snake-oil salesmen, health-food cranks, and medical quacks, the sales of herbal remedies such as St. John's wort, echinacea, and ginkgo biloba have doubled in the past ten years?

You can get even closer to readers by becoming more informal and intimate by using contractions, slang, and short, simple words. Informal writing often includes exclamations, deliberate sentence fragments, and short sentences as well:

It's hard to believe, but **it's** true. In just ten short years, the sales of herbal remedies such as St. John's wort, echinacea, and ginkgo biloba have doubled! **Why? Because television snake-oil salesmen, health-food cranks, and medical quacks have been telling people it's good for their health.**

OR

This may surprise you, but twice as many herbal remedies such as St. John's wort, echinacea, and ginkgo biloba are sold today as ten years ago. **Twice as much!** And I'll tell you why. **It's** because people have **swallowed** what some **television snake-oil salesmen, health-food cranks, and medical quacks** have told them.

The more informal your writing becomes, the more it will sound as if you're speaking rather than writing. Whether you want to give your writing such an intimate tone depends on who your readers are, what your purpose is in writing for them, and how you feel about your subject.

❧ TONE IN LARGER CONTEXTS

So far you've been experimenting with tone in individual sentences. In your own writing, however, your sentences are always a part of a larger context, paragraphs, and whole drafts. Suppose, for instance, you wrote a paragraph about two memorable astronomical events:

Some astronomers feel that it is time for the U.S. government to create an outer-space early-warning system to detect large asteroids before they collide with earth. A 2.5-mile-wide asteroid orbited within 2.2 million miles of earth in 1992. Another space rock large enough to be seen on earthbound telescopes passed by later that same year. The smaller one was still big enough to destroy a major city, while the larger one could easily have ended human life on earth just as a collision with an asteroid may have led to the dinosaurs' extinction. The purpose of the early-detection system would be to alert the government in time to launch rockets with atomic devices to destroy or deflect the invading asteroid. It is not certain, however, if any system could be accurate enough to detect a potential collision in time to allow for a rocket launch; both near misses in 1992 were discovered only after the asteroids had passed by. Nevertheless, the astronomers feel it is time for some action to be taken.

This is the kind of paragraph that a journalist, trying not to express her personality, might write to report the facts. That is, you didn't indicate, through word choice, sentence structure, or selection of details, either approval or disapproval of the astronomers' proposal. But you did try to suggest, especially through formal wording and the complete absence of humor, that the situation is important enough to be taken seriously by readers.

Given a different audience or a different mood, you might revise the paragraph to make the situation seem less serious—even to poke fun at the alarmist astronomers:

Some worrywart astronomers feel it is time for the U.S. government to create an outer-space early-warning system to detect large asteroids before they smash our little old planet to smithereens. One big bruiser of an asteroid whizzed by within a measly 2.2 million miles of the planet in 1992—to a lonely astronomer, that's the equivalent of a slow dance in terms of distance. Another piece of space debris large enough to be seen on earthbound telescopes—about the size of TV's Drew Carey and his coworker Mimi doing that slow dance—scooted past later that same year. The smaller one was still big enough to destroy a major city, while the larger could have easily made humans the dinosaurs of the modern age—fossil city in an instant. The purpose of the early-detection system would be to alert our government to launch rockets with atomic bombs—sort of paranoid welcome wagons—which would surely blow up the space invaders. Not! Because no one is certain we can build any system accurate enough to detect a potential collision in time to launch the rockets. "By the way," the astronomers tell us, "we noticed those near misses in 1992 only *after* the asteroids had passed by." Oh, great. Like getting onto the dance floor while the band is taking its break. Thanks for the terrific idea, guys!

The revised paragraph has a satirical tone, a tone that indicates that readers should not take the situation seriously. One sentence describes the scientists as **some worrywart astronomers,** making it seem as if they are few in number and slightly out of control of their emotions. The asteroids **whizzed by** and **scooted past,** informal language that minimizes the seriousness of their movement past our planet. Several sentences make jokes in order to diminish the importance of the subject—notice the reference to a **lonely astronomer** and **a slow dance** and to the extinction of the human race as **fossil city in an instant.** Calling the 2.5-mile-wide asteroid a **big bruiser** makes it seem less threatening and devalues the 2.2 million miles by describing it as **measly;** it also belittles the astronomers' concerns by comparing the asteroids to comic TV characters. The informal sentence structure makes the paragraph almost conversational (notice the sentence fragment **Not!**). Finally, referring to the astronomers as **guys** undermines all respect for them. Clearly, readers have little to worry about; it's time for a smile and a chuckle at someone else's expense.

Of course, it's quite possible to view the destruction of our planet as a matter of great concern. In that case, rather than creating a satirical tone by poking fun, you could decide to be more formal and add details that make clear the seriousness of the situation, as in the next paragraph:

> A number of concerned astronomers argue that it is time for the U.S. government to take action and create an outer-space early-warning system to detect large asteroids before they collide with earth. In 1992, a 2.5-mile-wide asteroid skimmed closer to the earth than our nearest planetary neighbor. Another piece of space debris large enough to be seen on earthbound telescopes passed by later that same year. The smaller one was 100 yards wide, massive enough to destroy a city the size of Cleveland, while the larger one could easily have extinguished human life on earth just as a collision with an asteroid ended the 65-million-year reign of earth's most successful animals: the dinosaurs. The astronomers' hope is that the early-detection system will alert the government in time to launch rockets with atomic devices to destroy or deflect the space intruders. Unfortunately, scientists cannot be certain that a detection system will be accurate enough to allow time for a preventive launch. Both near misses in 1992 were discovered only after the asteroids had threatened our planet and passed by. Still, now is the time to begin searching for solutions to the potential threat posed by our neighbors in space.

There is nothing amusing or satirical in this paragraph; in fact, the tone has become quite serious. Notice how the astronomers become respectable scientists with a serious view: **a number of concerned astronomers.** Their position is a stronger one as they now **argue** rather than **feel.** Vivid words convey the degree of danger to our planet: the asteroids **skimmed** the earth; the smaller asteroid was **massive;** human life might have been **extinguished;**

the asteroids **threatened** the earth; such threatening asteroids are close enough to be **neighbors.** The added details heighten the sense of importance of the astronomers' concern by suggesting that a collision might occur during the readers' lifetime, by naming a familiar city that the smaller asteroid might have destroyed, by showing how close the asteroid came to earth, and by emphasizing that even the long reign of the dinosaurs came to an abrupt end after an asteroid collision. Finally, the paragraph's last sentence emphasizes that humans need to act now to protect ourselves from the danger.

But you can approach the topic in yet another tone: anger. The next paragraph indicates that the public should mistrust the astronomers, whose poorly thought-out response overlooks other important issues:

> A few panic-stricken astronomers feel it is time for the U.S. government to create an outer-space early-warning system to detect large asteroids before they collide with earth. Of course, it isn't earth they want to save; it's their own skins, whatever the cost. Evidently, two asteroids sailed by earth in 1992, both large enough and close enough to cause grave concern. The purpose of the early-detection system would be to alert our government in time to launch rockets with atomic devices to destroy or deflect any alien visitor. But no one is certain about the effects of atomic detonations in outer space. Would the explosions cause damage to earth? If they did destroy these asteroids, what damage would the debris cause? Not only have the astronomers ignored these issues, but they also cannot be sure whether any system could provide a warning in time for a preventive launch; both asteroids in 1992, after all, were discovered only after they had passed by. And, of course, the astronomers assume that the United States needs to police the galaxy. This kind of ill-conceived alarmist reaction serves no useful purpose, promising only to gamble with taxpayers' money and perhaps worsen the situation the scientists hope to address.

Here you minimize the threat of collision, not to poke fun at it but to raise some other issues of importance. So the first sentence criticizes the astronomers **(panic-stricken astronomers)**, making them seem to be in a minority **(a few** rather than **several** or **a number of).** The phrase **sailed by** diminishes the threat posed by the asteroids by suggesting that they weren't very close. Notice that the details about the damage the asteroids might have caused is referred to in a very general way **(both large enough and close enough to cause grave concern).** This general reference allows the paragraph to emphasize other considerations such as the potential cost to the environment and to taxpayers. Anger is clear in the belittling comment about the astronomers' motivations: **saving their own skins, whatever the cost.** The phrase **gamble with taxpayers' money** suggests the unlikelihood of such a collision. The bitter use of **after all** and **only** questions the astronomers' ability to find threatening asteroids before they pose a threat. Asking questions but providing no answers also points out the shortcomings of the astronomers' views.

These four paragraphs about a potential threat to earth illustrate how you use words, phrases, and sentences in context to create tone. When you consider your purpose in each paragraph (to inform readers of a serious problem, to satirize an alarmist overreaction, to create a sense of urgent need to address a potential crisis, to criticize astronomers as untrustworthy), it affects the tone. But so does your awareness of your audience (readers in need of information, readers who might be fooled by the astronomers, readers who may have underestimated the problem, readers who may trust an untrustworthy group of experts) and your own attitudes toward the subject (it's a serious issue; it's an important problem; it's desperately vital; it's a deceptive situation). The point is that you can change the tone of your writing by increasing your awareness of why you are writing and for whom.

❧ PLAYING WITH TONE

In the next few pages, you'll have an opportunity to play with sentences and paragraphs, controlling, creating, and changing their tone. Remember what you've learned in the first half of this lesson as you combine the sentences in the exercises that follow. Focus not only on creating an appropriate tone for the purpose, intended readers, and writer's attitude toward the topic, but also on the need to create a consistent tone throughout your writing.

EXERCISES

Controlling and Creating Tone

Each of the following paragraphs has a particular tone. By using different words, reconstructing sentences, adding and omitting details, or making any other changes, rewrite each paragraph to give it the tone suggested by the directions.

EXAMPLE

The fuss about whether a century begins at the year 00 or at 01 goes back to a sixth-century monk and calendar maker by the name of Dionysius Exiguus, also known as Dennis the Short. The monk left one number out of his calendar—the number zero. He assigned the number 1, not 0, to the year he calculated as Christ's birth. It's hard to blame Dionysius, since European mathematics hadn't yet invented the concept zero. Nonetheless, if we follow his system, the years 1 to 101 make a century: 100 is part of the first century. The year 1800 correctly belongs in the eighteenth century, 2000 in the twentieth century. Oddly, it probably doesn't matter which view we follow, since the medieval monk made another mistake: he miscalculated the date of Christ's birth. According to the biblical account, Herod feared the birth of Jesus. Since Herod died in 4 B.C., the twenty-first century must have begun in 1996. [Rewrite the paragraph to make it more sarcastic.]

Why the fuss about whether a century begins at the year 00 or at 01? It goes back to a sixth-century monk named Dionysius Exiguus, also known as Dennis the Short. History doesn't record Dennis's actual height, but the monk was short one number in his calendar—the number zero. Little Dennis assigned the number 1 to the year he calculated as Christ's birth. Whether you blame him or not—European mathematics hadn't yet invented the concept zero—we follow his system. So the years 1 to 101 make a century. The first century includes the year 100, the year 1800 correctly belongs in the eighteenth century, 2000 in the twentieth century. Well, maybe not. It seems that the little monk made another mistake: the date of Christ's birth. Since the biblical account says that Herod feared the birth of Jesus, Christ couldn't have been born before Herod died. But Herod died in 4 B.C. Good grief! Thanks to Little Dennis's big goof, we didn't celebrate the beginning of the twenty-first century: January 1, 1996.

A. An inability to spell could cost you your self-respect. Psychologists believe that spelling ability has little to do with basic intelligence, yet poor spellers are viewed as ignorant or sloppy in their writing even though the true cause of poor spelling may be dyslexia or just our inconsistent English language. Some people turn desperately for help to computer spell-checking programs, which unfortunately cannot decide whether the writer means *there, their,* or *they're.* Others hold out for an impossible future of simplified spellings like *thru* for *through* or *hav* for *have.* In the end, spelling will always be a way to exclude and distinguish—those who can spell are "in," those who can't are "out." [Rewrite the paragraph to make the tone more playful and optimistic.]

B. Over 100 million acres of farmland were planted with genetically modified organisms (GMOs) in 2000, twenty-five times more than just four years earlier. GMOs are crops genetically altered to do things such as release their own insecticide or withstand the spraying of weed-killing chemicals. Proponents say GMO can increase crop yields, farm efficiency, and agricultural productivity. Opponents say that tampering with nature can inadvertently alter species, harm wildlife, and give rise to new problems like superweeds. Current statistics indicate that genetically modified crops are spreading so rapidly that it has become almost impossible to avoid them. Wind-blown pollen, mixed seeds, and black-market plantings have further extended these GMOs irreversibly into the world's food supply. One expert said, "The genie is out of the bottle, and it can't be put back in." [Rewrite the paragraph to make the tone less neutral and more negative in criticizing the growing use of GMOs.]

C. Each year, fraternities and sororities subject potential new members to a demeaning process that begins as *rush* and concludes with *hazing.* Supposedly a series of open houses and parties for the purpose of making friends and learning about the Greek system, rush is above all else a screening process for weeding out unacceptable pledges. It is a procedure whose escapades are bound by tradition, allowing the victims to be closely scrutinized in a variety of embarrassing and sometimes dangerous social situations. During hazing, the brothers and sisters humiliate the newcomers, from the first beer bash through the final dinner party, seeking people who are willing to make fools of themselves for the sake of acceptance. These mindless carbon copies of themselves are tendered an invitation to join the fraternal organization after Hell Night, the traditional climactic close of rush activities. [Rewrite the paragraph to make the tone more favorable toward fraternities and sororities.]

Eager Beavers

Revise the following sentences into an informative story that describes a common forest creature. By selecting from the words in parentheses, try to create a consistent tone, one that seems appropriate to the subject and that conveys some excitement about the unique anatomical feature most identified with the beaver. You may add or delete details as well as provide your own word choices for the sentences.

1. The beaver's unique tail makes it (fabulous, suitable, effective) for so many purposes.

2. The beaver's unique tail serves its owner as a (spectacular, personalized, virtual) tool kit.

3. The beaver (alerts, sends a wake-up call to, notifies) the colony of danger with its tail.

4. The beaver (flaps, slams, hits) its tail against the water surface.

5. The tail makes a loud (noise, "ka-whop," smack).

6. The loud (noise, "ka-whop," smack) echoes across the pond's still waters.

7. The beaver spends (many happy hours, much of its waking time, a lot of time) swimming.

8. The beaver (waggles, uses, positions) its wide tail as a rudder while swimming in order to move side to side.

9. The beaver (wiggles, uses, positions) its wide tail as a diving plane while swimming in order to move up and down.

10. During times of famine, the beaver can (live off, fall back on, rely upon) its tail as an emergency food supply.

11. The beaver's tail is very (fatty, tasty, filled with nutrients).

12. The tail is (hairless, bald, smooth as a baby's behind).

13. The tail serves as a(n) (air-conditioning unit, heat exchange mechanism, personal fan).

14. This happens when the beaver is (hyped up, on the go, extremely active).

15. The tail can (help out the beaver, stand in, serve) as a brace or prop.

16. The beaver sits up on its tail and (chomps on, gnaws, snacks on) trees in order to fell them.

17. Clearly, the beaver's tail is (very valuable, indispensable, absolutely a got-to-have) to its owner.

18. This (very valuable, indispensable, absolutely a got-to-have) tool is, fortunately, easy to carry.

19. It goes everywhere with its owner.

Revising for a Consistent Tone

Each of the paragraphs below is confusing because its tone is inconsistent. Following the specific directions, make the feelings and attitudes clear by revising each paragraph to create a more consistent tone.

EXAMPLE

Machiavelli is often blamed for originating the unwholesome opinion that the end justifies the means. Now, true, he would have his prince friends sock it good and hard to anyone challenging their power. But, really, he didn't mean for rulers to do whatever they pleased no matter who got hurt. In a world where wickedness and intrigue abounded, he was trying to teach some practical skills in governing well. Princes, he reasoned, should be good guys, upholding values such as truth, humanity, and religion, but they should also be ready to play the "fox" and lower the boom when necessary. Did the end justify the means for Machiavelli? Yeah, sort of, but he also saw the necessity for limiting those means. [Rewrite the paragraph to make the tone more consistent and mature.]

Machiavelli is often blamed for the controversial view that the end justifies the means. While he advised princes to be firm with those challenging their power, he prescribed limits for that firmness. In a world where wickedness and intrigue abounded, he was trying to teach some practical skills in governing well. Princes, he argued, should uphold values such as truth, humanity, and religion, but they should also be ready to play the "fox" or assert their authority when necessary. Thus the end justified the means for Machiavelli, but he also saw the necessity for limiting those means.

A. True to itself, the government obviously resorts to paranoid secrecy whenever its agencies conduct research that the public has good reason to suspect is either cruel or unethical. Since dogs are only animals, why not let them suffer? The Army has secretly subjected pooches to torture-endurance tests and, in the 1950s, hid from the public its testing of LSD and other dangerous drugs on unsuspecting American soldiers. I can't believe that they would do anything like that. Not to be outdone, even the Department of Transportation has admitted using human bodies in auto crash tests for years to study the effectiveness of air bags. I tend to believe, and so do many of my buddies that I've talked with, that it would be in the public interest for the government to announce the nature and purposes of any experiment that might conceivably prove questionable. [Rewrite the paragraph to eliminate the immaturity that makes the tone inconsistently sarcastic.]

B. Ever hear of Ts-ai Lun or Rene de Réaumur? Ts-ai Lun lived over 2,000 years ago in China while de Réaumur lived in the 1700s in Europe. What did these two folks have in common? They are two of the most significant figures in the development of paper. Ts-ai Lun ground up a collection of various fibers, such as mulberry bark, hemp, and linen, and stretched it out on a mat with a bamboo frame to dry in the sun. It must have looked like one great big mess, but he knew what he was doing. He had reasoned that he could make woven mats out of plant fibers that had been separated and suspended in water. Centuries later, de Réaumur noticed a bunch of bugs chomping away on wood, spitting out the chewed up glop, and forming nests with it. Pretty interesting, he thought. Stuff looks like paper. Although he never actually made paper out of wood, de Réaumur, like Ts-ai Lun, recorded his observations. Later on people used his ideas to make paper out of wood pulp. And if it weren't for this little history of a bunch of smushed-up plants, some hungry wasps, and two pretty smart fellows, you'd be reading this book on a clay tablet or a piece of tree bark. [Rewrite the paragraph to give it a consistent voice, decide whether to make the tone formal and serious or informal and playful.]

C. No one has ever proven that a brontosaurus-like monster inhabits Scotland's Loch Ness, but several people have tried. In 1934 the Loch Ness Monster was photographed by a London physician named Robert Wilson. Self-styled photographic experts have recently proven Wilson's picture to be fake, a set-up scene made from a small model of the lake and the monster. In the last twenty years, several tourists have video-taped snakelike objects undulating through the water. Strangely, their videos, all taken at night, are grainy and indistinct. Wouldn't you know? Sonar provides the best evidence for the monster's existence. In 1992, a sonar-equipped ship made contact with something moving in the lake at a depth of about 100 meters. But even the experts can't tell whether the something was a sea serpent or a large fish. [Rewrite the paragraph to make it consistently sarcastic.]

Choose Me

Selecting from the facts below, construct two pieces of writing, each no longer than 200 words. By revising the structure and diction in any way you choose, make sure that your first version is a suitable autobiographical statement as described in A. Make your second version into an appropriate letter to a new roommate as described in B.

> **A.** A required autobiographical statement to accompany your application for a college scholarship.
>
> **B.** A letter to your new college roommate. The purpose of your letter is to introduce yourself.
>
> **1.** I am eighteen years old and have just graduated from Feurtado High.
>
> **2.** I applied to four other colleges: Beloit College, University of Minnesota, Purdue University, and East Carolina University.
>
> **3.** I plan to major in history.
>
> **4.** I played the clarinet in my high school orchestra, and I received the music award in my senior year.
>
> **5.** In my junior year, I starred in my school's production of the play *Our Town.*
>
> **6.** I jog daily, and I occasionally play tennis and volleyball.
>
> **7.** My favorite sports are swimming and water skiing.
>
> **8.** I broke both my ankles last fall.
>
> **9.** To relax outdoors, I like to read travel or history books under a tree and to go fishing at the creek; to relax indoors, I play Ping Pong and watch TV. My favorite programs are *60 Minutes, Friends,* and *Biography.*
>
> **10.** Sponsored by Buzz Auffenneuter's Central Electronics, I participated in a dance marathon last year which raised $235 for the volunteer firefighters' fund.
>
> **11.** I am allergic to cats.
>
> **12.** I founded the Young Historians Club, and I edited the only issue of the club magazine *Historiana.*
>
> **13.** I was recently named president of the local chapter of the Young Democrats. Last fall, I campaigned in my neighborhood for State Representative Chin.
>
> **14.** For the past three summers, I've supervised the delivery and distribution of magazines, newspapers, and paperback books for Edna's News and Novelties.

15. My analysis of Lincoln's Gettysburg Address, entitled "A Mirror for Gettysburg: Lincoln and His Archetypes," won the annual R. F. Davis Award for the best essay by a senior.

16. I like to dance to all kinds of music as long as it has a beat.

17. I don't smoke.

18. One of my goals is to teach high school history; another is to enter local politics and eventually run for the state senate.

19. I do not intend to marry and settle down until after I have earned my college degree.

20. I have an older brother, Vince, who lives in Detroit, and two younger sisters, Alice and Connie, who live at home and attend junior high school.

21. Based on my past performance, my teachers and coaches predict success for me in the future. They often compliment me on my diligence, my perseverance, and my good sense.

22. I not only love hot Mexican food, but spicy Thai food is my newest dining passion.

Paragraph Patterns

Preview

All the structures and strategies we discuss in this book occur not only in writing but also in speech—except paragraphs. Paragraphs exist only in writing. They are necessary both to help readers follow a text and to help writers support and develop an essay's controlling idea. Since each paragraph begins with white space that a writer creates by indenting or skipping a line, a new paragraph provides a brief rest for the reader's eye and brain. Even more important, the start of a new paragraph signals the reader that a change is taking place—perhaps in place or time, perhaps from one idea to another or from a generalization to an example, perhaps from the body of an essay to its conclusion.

In explanatory and persuasive writing, paragraphs generally develop a controlling idea; they also help to inform or persuade the reader. Of all the ways you might organize explanatory paragraphs, four are especially useful: the direct pattern, the climactic pattern, the turnabout pattern, and the interrogative pattern. This lesson explores those four explanatory paragraph patterns.

The direct pattern states a controlling idea in its opening sentence and illustrates that controlling idea in the following sentences. The climactic paragraph inverts the structure of a direct paragraph, building a series of illustrations to the topic sentence, which comes at the end. The turnabout paragraph states one view in its opening sentence, then "turns" to a different view. The interrogative paragraph draws the reader into a controlling idea by asking a question that is answered later in the paragraph. The direct paragraph occurs more often than the rest, and it works the best for informing or clarifying. The others can often be more effective for persuading. They also add variety and drama to your writing.

❧ THE DIRECT PARAGRAPH

The DIRECT PARAGRAPH opens with a direct statement of its controlling idea, called a *topic sentence*. The sentences after the opening develop the paragraph's controlling idea by defining it, qualifying it, analyzing it, and—

most frequently—illustrating it. For example, in an anthropology class, you might have collected the following information on how people wait in line in different countries:

> In Arab countries, where women do not have equal rights, men commonly cut in front of women at ticket windows.
>
> In Britain and the United States, where "first come, first served" is almost an obsession, many businesses have customers take numbers to ensure that "first come" is really "first served."
>
> In southern Europe, where people don't like businesses regulating their behavior, lines are disorderly, with lots of pushing and shoving for the best position; the strongest or most aggressive win.

Since each of these sentences illustrates an unstated central point—that the way people wait in line reflects cultural values about fairness and equality—you can write a direct paragraph, with this central point as the opening sentence:

> **Anthropologists who study line-forming behavior have concluded that the way people wait in line reflects cultural values about fairness.** In Arab countries, where women do not have equal rights, men commonly cut in front of women at ticket windows. In Britain and the United States, where "first come, first served" is almost an obsession, many businesses have customers take numbers to ensure that "first come" is really "first served." By contrast, in southern Europe, where people don't like businesses regulating their behavior, lines are disorderly, with lots of pushing and shoving for the best position; the strongest or most aggressive win.

If you want to "drive home" your controlling idea, you can use your final sentence to do more than add another illustration. In the next paragraph, the last sentence suggests an imaginary variation on actual omelettes in order to emphasize the controlling idea—that you can mix so many things with eggs:

> **The wonder of omelettes is that so many things can be put into them.** Take cheese, for example. All sorts of cheese, like Swiss or provolone, feta or mozzarella, slide deliciously into the omelette's fold, enhancing the texture of the eggs. And vegetables, from the predictable onions and green peppers to the less common spinach and kohlrabi, add vital flavor. Still more lavish, for those who are not vegetarians, is the addition of a meat, possibly pepperoni or bacon or ham. But the omelette's most exotic components might be the fruits that give it tang: raisins and avocados. **Maybe someday an enterprising chef will figure out how to mix liquor and candy with eggs to produce a vodka-and-fudge omelette.**

Another way to emphasize the controlling idea is by restating it in the final sentence. Restating the topic sentence is especially useful when your controlling idea is complex. In the following paragraph, the idea that the free road map is extinct relies on explaining how oil companies justify their changing priorities. To relate the two points more clearly, the writer states the main idea in the opening sentence and then repeats it in the closing sentence:

> **The free road map has become a fossil of an earlier age—a dinosaur killed by changing priorities.** At one time, service stations dispensed road maps as freely as they washed windshields. In the 1960s, one oil company official boasted that "free road maps are an institution peculiar to Americans." Well, the institution peaked in 1972 with the production of 250 million maps and then began its decline. If you ask for a road map in a service station today, you'll have to pay for it. Citing higher production costs and increased charges for foreign crude, oil companies claim that eliminating road maps was actually patriotic. After all, they explain, maps promote travel and travel burns fuel, increasing the nation's trade imbalance. **With this logic, it's no wonder that the free road map is extinct.**

The direct paragraph occurs more frequently than any other pattern. It has an obvious advantage over all other paragraph patterns: it is well suited to inform and clarify because, from the start, it lets readers know where they're going. For this reason, the direct paragraph minimizes the chances for misunderstanding. But while the direct paragraph is often the best pattern for informing and for clarifying, it is not always as effective for persuading as the other common paragraph patterns—the climactic paragraph, the turnabout paragraph, and the interrogative paragraph.

✌ THE CLIMACTIC PARAGRAPH

A CLIMACTIC PARAGRAPH is like a direct paragraph turned upside down. It begins with illustrations and closes with the topic sentence. In the paragraph below, for example, a series of comments about the hunting ability of cats appears before the controlling idea itself is actually stated in the concluding sentence:

> Cats, domestic or wild, are born with the instinct to hunt. Because their brains are wired to make stalking and attacking reflex actions, cats take what is known as a "stalk-and-pounce" approach to the hunt. They can even stalk birds, which have incredibly acute senses. They approach stealthily on padded paws, freeze in their tracks, and leap onto the prey

in a burst of explosive energy. Then they play with "prey," dead or alive. Felines are gifted with the tools and techniques needed to chase prey in the wild or toys in the living room—speed, stealth, and a killer instinct. **If you designed a "dream machine" for hunting, you'd come up with something very close to a cat.**

The climactic paragraph tends to be more persuasive than the direct paragraph because the pattern of the climactic paragraph corresponds more closely to the pattern of much of our thinking: we often begin by collecting data—an example or two here, an instance or two there—until we have enough evidence to make a generalization or reach a conclusion. At its best, the climactic paragraph leads your readers, step-by-step, to a conclusion that seems to follow naturally from the examples and illustrations. Notice what happens when you make the direct paragraph about standing in line into a climactic paragraph by moving the topic sentence to the end:

In Arab countries, where women and men do not have equal rights, men commonly cut in front of women at ticket windows. In Britain and the United States, where "first come, first served" is almost an obsession, many businesses have customers take numbers to ensure that "first come" is really "first served." By contrast, in southern Europe, where people don't like businesses regulating their behavior, lines are disorderly, with lots of pushing and shoving for the best position; the strongest or most aggressive win. **Anthropologists who study line-forming behavior have concluded that the way people wait in line reflects cultural values about fairness.**

By withholding the statement of the controlling idea until the end, you build an element of surprise and drama into this climactic version. You also prepare your readers, one illustration at a time, for the idea you want them to accept—the controlling idea in the final sentence.

❧ THE TURNABOUT PARAGRAPH

Unlike direct or climactic paragraphs, which move in one direction only, TURNABOUT PARAGRAPHS first move in one direction and then "turn about" in another. The turnabout paragraph begins with an idea that is often the opposite of its controlling idea. That is, if the topic sentence of a turnabout paragraph states that "ballet dancing demands as much strength, stamina, and athletic skill as professional football," the paragraph is likely to begin by suggesting the opposite: "Most people wouldn't equate the National Football League players who slam and bash each other on Sunday afternoons with American Ballet Theatre dancers who perform in *Swan Lake* and *The*

Nutcracker." The turnabout paragraph below, which develops the controlling idea that "our genes determine who we are much more than does our environment," appropriately begins with a different idea:

> Most people believe that how we are brought up determines how we will act. We think that environment plays a greater role in determining our personalities than inherited characteristics. But psychologists studying identical twins separated at birth and raised in different households suggest otherwise. They point to story after story of separated twins who lived strangely similar lives. Take the "Jim Twins," for instance, who did not meet until age thirty-nine. Each had married a woman named Linda. Each had owned a boyhood dog named Toy. Each worked as a deputy sheriff. They had done well in the same subjects at school and even shared a common slang. Repeated stories like this have led researchers to claim that **our genes determine who we are much more than does our environment.**

To signal readers that your turnabout paragraph may not be leading them where they expect, you generally suggest that the first statement may not be correct, and then you mark the turn clearly. As another aid to readers, you often conclude a turnabout paragraph with a statement or restatement of its controlling idea. The turnabout paragraph below employs all three ways to help the reader follow its movement. The word **resembles** in the first sentence encourages readers to doubt the comparison of the Mall of America to other malls. The word **but** in the fifth sentence forcefully signals the turnabout. And the final sentence clearly states the controlling idea—that the Mall is actually a huge tourist attraction:

> The Mall of America in Minneapolis **resembles** other large suburban malls. It has stores like Macy's, B. Dalton, and Sears. It cocoons shoppers from the harsher elements. Its air temperature remains a constant seventy degrees all year long. It even has a problem with teenagers. **But** the huge Mall of America is much more than a mall. Besides more stores, it has an amusement park, a 12-million-gallon aquarium, and an eighteen-hole miniature-golf course. The shopping and novelties bring this huge mall 42 million visitors a year from as far away as Osaka and Amsterdam. **And that makes the Mall of America the most successful tourist attraction in America, attracting more visitors than Disney World, the Grand Canyon, and Graceland combined.**

Carefully constructed turnabout paragraphs tend to be persuasive. If you want to persuade or move your reader from one idea to another, then the turnabout paragraph may be the most effective pattern. Because it presents one point of view before advancing another, the turnabout paragraph suggests that you have examined both sides of an issue. Once you have convinced your readers of your sense of fairness, you will find them more willing to accept your viewpoint.

৵ THE INTERROGATIVE PARAGRAPH

The INTERROGATIVE PARAGRAPH differs from the other types of explanatory paragraphs because it opens with a question. The opening question is used either as an introduction to the controlling idea or as a transition from one idea to the next. The opening question of the following paragraph introduces the controlling idea, that de Camp's book **explores what many consider the "secrets" of the ancients, which turn out not to be so secret after all:**

> **Have you ever wondered how ancient peoples accomplished such marvelous feats of engineering as the Egyptian pyramids, the Great Wall of China, and the fabled Tower of Babylon?** If you have, then you should read *The Ancient Engineers*, by L. Sprague de Camp. **The book explores what many consider the "secrets" of the ancients, which turn out not to be so secret after all.** While the ancient Egyptians, Chinese, and Babylonians did not have engineering know-how equivalent to ours, they were able to make optimal use of what they did know, largely because they had an unlimited source of labor and—what may be more important—infinite patience. De Camp discloses that the Egyptians used 100,000 slave laborers over a twenty-year period to build the Great Pyramid. He also shows that the Chinese labored for centuries on the Great Wall, as did the Babylonians on the Tower.

Because questions have a strong psychological hold on human beings, paragraphs that begin with a question tend to involve readers more directly in writing than do other paragraph patterns. Notice how the opening sentence of the next paragraph almost gets you responding silently, with your own question, "OK, why *do* track coaches watch so carefully as students walk by in the corridors?" The opening question not only introduces you to the controlling idea but also demands your response:

> **Why do high school track coaches watch so carefully as students walk by in the corridors? To look for youngsters who are pigeon-toed, bow-legged, or flat-footed, of course.** It seems that such youngsters make the best sprinters. Coaches know that a normal gait, with toes pointed outward, slows people down. A normal gait forces the heels to slip forward as the body raises up on the toes, detracting from the force of the pushoff. Those odd gaits, though, give runners a firmer landing and kickoff, producing faster sprinters.

Like the turnabout paragraph, the interrogative paragraph can help you persuade your readers to accept your viewpoint. For instance, if you want to convince your readers to take up jogging, you might try an opening question like this: "Would you like to firm up flabby muscles, lose weight, handle stress better, and have more energy, too?" Before they can read the next sentence in your paragraph, "Then you should take up jogging," many of your readers will be responding affirmatively to your question and will be more open to your point of view.

ᵅ PLAYING WITH PARAGRAPH PATTERNS

Since paragraphs exist only in writing, not speaking, writers who can skillfully control paragraph structures are considered artful writers, writers who know what they are doing. The ability to use the paragraph patterns explained in this lesson—direct paragraphs, turnabout paragraphs, climactic paragraphs, and interrogative paragraphs—will allow you to write prose that readers consider skillful and well crafted. Remember to use them in your own writing, along with the other structures and strategies you've learned in this book.

EXERCISES

Constructing Paragraph Patterns

The sentences are out of order in the groups below. Read through them to get the sense of their meaning. Then organize each group of sentences into an effective paragraph of the pattern indicated. Be sure to write out each paragraph.

EXAMPLE: HOW TO MAKE A DESERT

Organize these sentences into a *turnabout* paragraph.

1. It is almost a cliché to blame modern industrial growth for the destruction of the natural environment.

2. This process of "desertification" destroyed three-fourths of the forest land in Argentina in fifty years, and one-third of the farmland in western India in a single decade.

3. However, we sometimes overlook the damage done by less sophisticated means.

4. Every year, cattle and sheep farmers in nonindustrial societies turn nearly 17 million acres of land into desert by overgrazing.

5. Unchecked industrial growth may pollute the air, but unscientific herd management ravages the land.

↓

It is almost a cliché to blame modern industrial growth for the destruction of the natural environment. However, we sometimes overlook the damage done by less sophisticated means. Unchecked industrial growth may pollute the air, but unscientific herd management ravages the land. Every year, cattle and sheep farmers in nonindustrial societies turn nearly 17 million acres of land into desert by overgrazing. This process of "desertification" destroyed three-fourths of the forest land in Argentina in fifty years and one-third of the farmland in western India in a single decade.

Name Calling

Organize these sentences into a *direct* paragraph.

198

1. There was a time when parents honored their newborn children by naming them after figures in the Old Testament, like Esther and Ezekiel.

2. During the years following World War II, most parents thought twice before naming a son Adolph or a daughter Rose, lest they be associated with Adolf Hitler or Tokyo Rose.

3. Like clothing and hairstyles, the naming of children has always reflected the fads and fancies of culture.

4. And when President Nixon resigned from office rather than risk impeachment for Watergate–related crimes, it's a safe bet that the name Richard became less popular.

5. Back in seventeenth-century Ireland, after the Protestant army of William III defeated the Catholic army of James II, loyal Catholic parents stopped naming boys William.

6. The fashion passed, but parents have continued to be influenced—often negatively—by the reputations of famous men and women.

On Ice

Organize these sentences into a *turnabout* paragraph.

1. Players feel pressured by their organization to put on a spectacular show, a practice that translates into more violence.

2. We assume that players almost instinctively react to a push or a shove with fists flying.

3. In fact, one team's publicity agent admitted that his organization stresses violence as a major attraction to spectators.

4. Yet, according to a Canadian criminologist who has studied fighting in hockey games, violence reflects not the killer instincts of players but the greedy policies of owners.

5. Violence is so common in hockey that we can't help believing that players crave nothing more than a good fight.

Bigfoot

Organize these sentences into a *climactic* paragraph.

1. Despite its variety of names, in every case it is an eight- to ten-foot-tall man-ape, a strange and hairy being that flees at the sight of humans.

2. In the Pacific Northwest, where it roams the great forest, it is commonly called Bigfoot.

3. Native Americans refer to it as Sasquatch, which means "the wild man of the woods."

4. Whether the creature exists or not, the proliferation of stories about it surely points to a human need to believe in the strange, the mysterious, the unknown.

5. To the Russians, it is the final descendant of the Neanderthals and is known as Alma.

6. In Nepal, it is Yeti, the Abominable Snowman, a feared yet revered creature who wanders in the snows of the Himalayas.

Poets

Organize these sentences into an *interrogative* paragraph.

1. In the nineteenth century, poetry was just about the most popular literature, and some poets—like Byron, Shelley, Keats, and Tennyson—even became celebrities.

2. Can you associate the names Alberto Rios, Rita Dove, Denise Levertov, Billy Collins, or Galway Kinnell with an occupation?

3. In their own time, they were as well known as movie stars like Whoopi Goldberg, Julia Roberts, Matt Damon, and Will Smith are today.

4. But such was not always the case.

5. You probably don't know that Rios, Dove, Levertov, Collins, and Kinnell are among the most respected contemporary poets, because few people today read poetry or pay attention to living poets.

The Bear Facts

Revise the sentences below into an explanatory essay about how and why teddy bears became popular. Since this is a subject most of us can relate to personally, you may add details from your own experience that make the essay more engaging and more individual. Be sure to construct at least one paragraph like those discussed in this unit—direct, climactic, turnabout, or interrogative.

1. Winston Churchill, Radar O'Reilly, and Christopher Robin have something in common.

2. The great World War II leader was an arctophile.

3. The company clerk in *M*A*S*H* was an arctophile.

4. And the protagonist of the *Winnie the Pooh* books was an arctophile.

5. An arctophile is a lover of teddy bears.

6. And they're not the only teddy lovers.

7. This is so if recent statistics are a true indication of bear popularity.

8. The "bear" facts are these.

9. Toy bear sales rose to several hundred million per year in the 1980s.

10. Over 40 percent of those sales were to adults.

11. The teddy bear mania began with a hunting trip.

12. President Theodore Roosevelt took it in 1902.

13. It seems that [this happened].

14. The president refused to shoot a bear under unsportsmanlike conditions.

15. A political cartoon popularized the scene.

16. A Russian immigrant received permission from TR to call the stuffed bears *teddy bears.*

17. He sold the stuffed bears in his Brooklyn candy store.

18. He was named Morris Michton.

19. Michton eventually founded the Ideal Toy Corporation.

20. Bears may have become popular because [of this].

21. They were associated with a popular president.

22. But they have remained popular because [of this].

23. They fill a need in people's lives.

24. Bears are comforting to hug.

25. And bears are comforting to talk to.

26. So people of all ages learn to rely on them.

27. Olympic athlete Greg Louganis talked to his bear.

28. This was during his gold-medal dives at the Los Angeles Olympics.

29. Bears have accompanied fighter pilots.

30. Bears have traveled with Arctic explorers.

31. Bears have driven with daredevil racers.

32. And we all remember hugging our own teddies.

33. This was when things got tough at day care.

34. It is not unusual to rely on stuffed bears.

35. Marc Stutsky summed it up nicely.

36. Marc Stutsky is a noted psychiatrist.

37. He said teddies "make scary things manageable."

38. Life might be "unbearable" without stuffed animals.

Revising Paragraphs

The paragraphs below are written as either direct, climactic, turnabout, or interrogative patterns. Rewrite each as a different type, changing sentences where appropriate. Make sure you write out the complete paragraphs.

EXAMPLE

Is romance a thing of the past? It is, according to one Michigan State psychologist, who claims that romance is going out of our lives. According to him, the conditions for romantic love no longer exist, replaced in men and women today by a pragmatic cynicism in which they view each other with a cool and objective eye. He says that freer attitudes toward sex and contraception have also helped kill off romance. Would-be Dantes can have affairs with would-be Beatrices rather than mope and pine away in poetry. [Interrogative paragraph]

A Michigan State psychologist confirmed what most of us already know—that romance is going out of our lives and that the conditions for romantic love no longer exist. According to him, those conditions are replaced in men and women today by a pragmatic cynicism in which they view each other with a cool and objective eye. The psychologist claims that freer attitudes toward sex and contraception have also helped to kill off romance. It seems that would-be Dantes can now have affairs with would-be Beatrices rather than mope and pine away in poetry. [Direct paragraph]

A. In the quiet 1980s, students were supposedly dull and conforming. But they may in fact have been as imaginative and rebellious as their counterparts in the 1960s and 1970s, if the behavior of Cal Tech students is indicative. A group of them disassembled a senior's Porsche and left it in his room, completely reassembled and with the engine running. When McDonald's ran a promotional contest in California, Cal Tech students found a loophole in the rules and programmed a computer to spit out 1.2 million entries, winning thousands of dollars in prizes. A senior physics major created a quantum mechanics problem for some undergraduates as a prank and ended up with a puzzle that stumped even a Nobel Prize–winning physicist. Some dullards! Some conformists! [Turnabout paragraph]

B. There are two folk rock singers who are dedicated to their causes and have been since their first album, *Nomads Indians Saints*. Their powerfully poetic and profoundly meaningful lyrics deal with issues of spirituality, open-mindedness, and social responsibility. In particular, they advocate for people who have been relegated to the margins of our society—Native Americans, Latina women. Their song "Leeds" protests the arson of African American churches. Their Web site features this motto: "Rock is cool but the struggle is better . . ." These singers exemplify rock stars who use their popularity to increase their listeners' awareness of and support for important social issues. Indeed, the Indigo Girls are consummate musicians who possess more than just talent; they also have a conscience and a heart. [Climactic paragraph]

C. Have people really progressed since primitive times, or does civilization simply cover our innate savagery? A British Broadcasting Corporation documentary indicates that we may not be as civilized as we think. To film a documentary on life in the Iron Age, the BBC hired a group of ten men and ten women to live in an ancient village just outside Stonehenge. There, the men and women had to live as their distant ancestors did: they wove cloth, made tools, farmed in ancient ways, and practiced the Celtic religion. After a year, their behavior changed. They walked more slowly, and they talked more slowly. They slept longer and were less inhibited about nudity. They were more self-sufficient but also less civilized. At the planting ceremony, for instance, they forced one member of the group to be lashed as a sacrifice to ensure a good harvest. [Interrogative paragraph]

D. Electronic magazines, or e-zines, are a new wave of alternative press distributed on the Internet. Not meant for a mass audience, zines appeal instead to a specific, small segment of the population, such as skateboarders, ska band fans, or Gothic romance readers. Their animated graphics and interactive stories engage readers more than printed magazines. Rather than slavishly flipping pages, you click on an image or phrase to follow a line of thought you want to pursue. Most of the zines—since they are often bizarre, irreverent, nontraditional, and "in your face"—appeal to the young. But Internet watchers expect the field to grow and interest investors, educators, and gardeners as well as video game buffs. [Direct paragraph]

The Home Front

Revise the following sentences into an explanatory essay about how civilians lived during World War II and how they produced the weapons of war. Be sure to create at least one paragraph like those discussed in this unit—direct, climactic, turnabout, or interrogative. If you can, add details from movies or TV shows you've seen, from books you've read, or from what your parents or grandparents have told you about those times.

1. Large numbers of the civilian population took to the streets during the Vietnam War era.
2. [This happened] in protest against our most unpopular war.
3. Civilians stood firmly behind the government to help defeat Germany and Japan.
4. [This happened] a generation before the war in Vietnam.
5. [This happened] during World War II.

6. Most of the young men were in the military.
7. So women had to replace men in industrial jobs.

8. The women were symbolized by Rosie the Riveter.
9. The women left their homes to work in the factories.
10. Rosie the Riveter was a cartoon figure.
11. She wore coveralls and carried a pipe wrench.

12. And she urged workers to greater production.
13. Women like Rosie learned how to solder.
14. They learned how to run lathes.
15. And they learned how to rivet metal parts together.

16. The civilians on the homefront did without new cars.

17. They did without new refrigerators.

18. They put up with shortages of certain foods.

19. And they put up with shortages of luxury items.

20. They bought gas and tires only when they had saved enough ration coupons.

21. They carpooled to work in broken-down Studebakers and Nashes built before the war.

22. The civilians put up blackout curtains at night.

23. And they turned on the radio to hear Gabriel Heatter or H. V. Kaltenborn.

24. Heatter and Kaltenborn announced the latest news from the European and Pacific theaters of operation.

25. This was how millions of Americans spent the war years.

26. They were waiting for loved ones in uniform.

27. They were listening to the radio.

28. And they were taking part in the greatest production effort a people has ever made.

29. All the civilians pitched in.

30. Women like Rosie pitched in.

31. And men exempt from the draft pitched in.

32. High school kids spent evenings in tank factories and steel mills.

33. Old people in retirement took up half-forgotten trades.

34. Together they produced the weapons that fought the Axis.

35. They produced 296,029 airplanes.

36. They produced 86,333 tanks.

37. And they produced 319,000 artillery pieces.

38. They saved tin cans.

39. They brushed their teeth with half brushfuls of toothpaste.

40. And they volunteered their time at the local USO.

41. They walked the darkened streets in the evenings as air raid wardens.

42. Or they strained their eyes.

43. They peered through the night skies as aircraft-warning watchers.

44. They waited.

45. They worked.

46. They lined up for hard-to-get items.

47. Sugar was a hard-to-get item.

48. Nylon stockings were hard-to-get items.

49. And coffee was a hard-to-get item.

50. They were unlike the civilians during the Vietnam War.

51. They were a people united against a common enemy.

52. They were united in their desire to win a war they believed in.

Rewriting: Using Details

Preview

This lesson makes the points that good writing paints scenes with details that appeal to the senses. There are usually plenty of opportunities to show rather than tell, especially in the revision phase of the writing process. When you add details, you sharpen images, making your writing more vivid. When you convert *telling statements* into *showing statements,* you enable readers to share in your experiences, to see and hear and feel and taste and smell what you saw, heard, felt, tasted, and smelled.

✍ USING DETAILS TO PAINT A PICTURE

We say that a picture is worth a thousand words because a picture paints a scene—its color, shape, and texture. But writing can paint scenes, too. In fact, good writing is alive with details that capture the sights, sounds, smells, tastes, and textures of the real world. That's why, when you finish a book you enjoyed reading, you often remark, "It was so real that I felt I was there." Details make writing interesting and engaging and give it life.

Read the following draft of a young woman's reactions to meeting her blind date.

First Impressions

I learned one day that you can never trust your first impressions. Sarah had set me up on a blind date with Benny. I didn't really want to go, but when I talked to him on the phone, he seemed nice enough, so I agreed.

I was all dressed up and thinking we'd be going somewhere nice. That's what he had told me on the phone. I was all nervous because I didn't know what he looked like, what he would be like, or if he would even like me. It was really hard for me to go out with a guy I didn't know.

When he finally got there, I saw that his car was old and rusty. It was really ugly. He walked up to my door, and I saw that he was not dressed very well, not at all as nicely as I was. It looked as if he needed a shower. I knew I had made a big mistake in agreeing to go on this date. He was obviously an insensitive slob. I was pretty sure we weren't going anywhere nice.

Just when I thought he was a big jerk, he opened the car door for me and told me that he was going to change his clothes before dinner. He was a really nice guy. I felt a lot better and thought that we would probably get along just fine. I was really wrong about him, based on my first impressions. It's true what they say: You can't judge a book by its cover!

After Melissa brought this first draft to her writing group, they helped her to see that she had not really created a vivid picture for her readers. So then she revised the draft. Read the new draft and notice all of the showing details she has added.

Beneath All That Rust

I heard his car before I actually saw it. My heart sank, and I wiped my sweating palms on my freshly pressed dress. I looked into the mirror and saw the worry in my own eyes, but other than that, my hair and makeup were perfect. As the chugging, pounding sound outside my house grew louder, I stared out the window at the rusted pile of car parts that was once an Oldsmobile 88. Benny, a boy I'd never met before and had only spoken to once on the phone, sat behind the wheel. As he turned off the engine, a huge black puff of smoke flew out of the exhaust. I stood my ground, paralyzed with shock at the thought of sitting inside that old rattletrap of an Olds.

Finally, Benny stepped out of the car. I went numb when I saw he was wearing a Baltimore Orioles cap, a tattered Lollapalooza T-shirt, cutoff shorts, and muddy work shoes. I looked conspicuously at my own new dress, stockings, and heels. I was way overdressed! I was sure the date would be a disaster, envisioning myself at the Seven-Eleven eating a frozen burrito and sipping daintily on a cherry slushy. Even so, when he knocked, I walked down the hall, like a prisoner trudging to certain death, and opened the door.

"Hey, Melissa," he said. "Ready to go?"

I blinked at him in response. I thought, I'm going to kill Sarah for setting me up on this blind date with Conan the Horrible.

"Gonna be a big night," he said and sauntered to the waiting Olds as I followed him, wondering why I had answered the door, wondering why I was going on this date.

Benny stopped abruptly in my path, standing before the passenger's door. I stopped as well, afraid he was going to spit tobacco or belch or do something equally disgusting before he drove me to the Seven-Eleven. He reached out and grasped the door handle. With a flourish, he creaked open the door and gestured me in.

"Sorry about the car!" he said sheepishly. "I'm trying to rebuild it, so I can sell it. But it's really clean inside."

Surprised at his sudden chivalry, I slid into the car. It smelled of sweet pine, and the old leather shone in the late afternoon sunlight. As he walked around the car, I noticed a dark sports coat in a dry-cleaning bag hanging over the backseat.

"I hope you don't mind. I need to swing by my place and shower and change. I just got off work, and I didn't want to be late." He gave me a brilliant smile, and for the first time, I noticed how cute he was.

"That's fine," I said. "Nice car."

"Thanks," he replied. With a clatter, we moved away from the curb. "Well, it's a work in progress, you could say. You never can tell what's underneath all that rust and rumbling."

I nodded and smiled. I knew exactly what he meant.

In "Beneath All That Rust" Melissa makes you feel as if you have been there with her. She evokes the scene better because her story is alive with vivid images. "First Impressions" lacks the specific details that would bring it to life for the reader. It *tells* us how the writer felt and what she did. It *tells* us that she was nervous and shy, that she was upset by her first impression of Benny and his car, that she felt the date was going to go poorly, and, finally, that she learned a lesson about making false judgments. But these generalizations are never made vivid enough for us to picture the scene; the draft is weak because of what it leaves out. We don't see or feel or hear what the writer saw or felt or heard, so we are left unsatisfied. We don't really know the details of what went on.

In "Beneath All That Rust," on the other hand, Melissa includes details that create a scene. Here is Benny's rusted-out, smoke-belching wreck of an old Olds pulling up outside Melissa's house. There is Melissa's horrified response to Benny's Orioles cap, concert T-shirt, cutoff shorts, and dirty work shoes. We share her nightmare vision of "dining out" on a "frozen burrito and . . . a cherry slushy" at the convenience store. We follow Melissa's trudging steps down the hall to answer the door and monitor her ever-deepening despair as she vows revenge on her friend Sarah for setting her up with a boy she colorfully describes as "Conan the Horrible." As they pause next to the car, we share her fear that her blind date is about to spit tobacco or belch, and along with Melissa, we hear the creaky car door open. Then we are as surprised as she is when Benny apologizes ("Sorry about the car") and explains himself ("I'm trying to rebuild it . . . it's really clean inside."). As Melissa slides into the car, we, too, smell the pine air freshener, see the shiny leather, and, most important, notice Benny's dry-cleaned sports coat in the back. As the draft concludes, Benny's comments about his car allow us to see what he is really like, at the same time *showing* us what Melissa has learned from her experience. "Beneath All That Rust" succeeds because the writer makes the characters and situations come alive with details that appeal to our senses and to our imagination: Melissa paints a picture with words.

✌ SHOW, DON'T TELL

As you can see by contrasting these two drafts, it's generally better to show than to tell. The writer of "Beneath All That Rust" doesn't tell us that Benny's car is a wreck. She lets us hear its "chugging" and "pounding" and shows us the "huge black puff of smoke" flying out of its exhaust. She doesn't have to tell us that she learned it isn't a good idea to base judgments on first impressions. She shows us the lesson through Benny's own comments about his car: "You never can tell what's underneath all that rust and rumbling." Melissa doesn't tell; she shows.

You can use the same technique. Do you want your readers to know that a character is nervous? Don't say, "He was nervous." Show us that his hand is wet and clammy when you shake it. Does your history prof smoke too much? Don't tell the readers. Show them that his clothes stink from tobacco and that his fingers are discolored by nicotine.

Both "First Impressions" and "Beneath All That Rust" are narrative papers. The same idea of showing applies to explanatory writing. Don't merely tell your reader that the United States is no longer the leader in proportion of the population with a college degree; show them that Norway, Great Britain, and the Netherlands all have a graduation rate of more than 34% while the United States has 32.9% (Source: *USA Today*, "USA Falls to Fourth in College Grad Rate," May 18, 2000). Don't inform your readers that too many movies in the 2000s have been noisy adaptations of computer video games. Show them this trend by describing such unimaginative films as *Mortal Kombat, Final Fantasy*, and *Lara Croft: Tomb Raider*.

✌ ADDING DETAILS TO SENTENCES

Showing sharpens and focuses impressions for your readers, sometimes by giving characteristics, sometimes by distinguishing parts, sometimes by making comparisons. You often start a sentence with a "telling" statement, then sharpen its focus by adding more details in the form of grammatical structures like participles, appositives, absolutes, and subordinate clauses. Notice the difference between the next two sentences:

What I first noticed when Zach walked in the door was his backpack.

↓

What I first noticed when Zach walked in the door was his backpack, **shiny new and bulging with books.**

The first sentence tells us that the writer noticed Zach's backpack, but we do not know what characteristics about the backpack caught her eye. In the second sentence, the phrase **shiny new and bulging with books** furnishes that information by giving characteristics of the bag.

In the next example, the writer first tells us that the sports announcer's approach to football was unorthodox. Then she rewrites it, narrowing the focus by adding modifiers that distinguish the parts of his unusual behavior. She shows us exactly what it was about his announcing that made her come to the conclusion that he was unorthodox:

There was something unorthodox about the way John Madden described a football game.

↓

There was something unorthodox about the way John Madden described a football game—**the way he rejoiced over dirty, bloody uniforms, the joy he showed in drawing arrows and circles illustrating a touchdown pass.**

Melissa uses this technique of adding focusing details to sentences several times in "Beneath All That Rust." As her blind date arrives, she tells us the date is going to be a failure—"I was sure the date would be a disaster." Then she shows us exactly what she means by a disaster by adding modifiers to this main clause:

I was sure the date would be a disaster, **envisioning myself at the Seven-Eleven eating a frozen burrito and sipping daintily on a cherry slushy.**

Sometimes the details you add to sentences can sharpen the focus by showing that one thing is like something else. Usually, you make comparisons with phrases that begin with **like** or **as:**

Sam and Marilyn scampered onto the playground, **like** puppies out on a romp.

The figure skater spun on a single blade, **as** still in motion **as** a top.

Melissa says she walked reluctantly to the door to meet her blind date **like a prisoner trudging to certain death.** Sometimes you can make the comparison by omitting the connecting word **like** or **as.** Notice in the following revision of the Sam and Marilyn sentence that the writer shows us how the two children behaved by omitting **like,** describing them as if they were puppies, not merely like them:

> Sam and Marilyn scampered onto the playground, **puppies out on a romp.**

You might think about using comparisons, with or without **like** or **as,** to add detail to your sentences.

In brief, you can sharpen and focus impressions in your writing by adding details that

- give characteristics or circumstances
- distinguish parts
- make comparisons

The following three sentences show each of these strategies at work:

1. Down the slope came Avis, **intent on keeping her balance.**
2. Down the slope came Avis, **her hands tightly clutching the ski poles.**
3. Down the slope came Avis, **as awkward as a newborn colt attempting to walk for the first time.**

✌ CHANGING TELLING STATEMENTS INTO SHOWING STATEMENTS

It's not always enough to add details to a sentence to make it more vivid and appealing. Sometimes you have to rewrite a telling statement to make it a showing statement. For example, the sentence "Shaquille O'Neal is unusually tall" becomes more memorable if you change it into "Shaquille O'Neal ducks his head whenever he comes through a door." When Melissa drafted "First Impressions," she missed an opportunity to show us how inappropriately her blind date was dressed when she wrote, "I saw that he was not dressed very well, not at all as nicely as I was." Notice how much more vividly she shows us Benny's appearance in "Beneath All That Rust": "He was wearing a Baltimore Orioles cap, a tattered Lollapalooza T-shirt, cutoff shorts, and muddy work shoes." It's that sort of writing that makes "Beneath All That Rust" so lively and interesting.

You can choose whether to show or tell, especially when you revise early drafts of your writing. What if you were writing about a trip that you and your mother had recently taken, and you wanted to indicate that the bellhop who carried your bags in a Denver hotel was courteous but not friendly? You could make a telling statement to that effect, leaving your readers to wonder what it was about the bellhop that made you think he was courteous but not friendly:

> A courteous but not friendly bellhop carried our bags to the room.

Or you could show what the bellhop did, letting the readers see the bellhop's actions and even hear him speak:

> "May I take your bags, sir?" the bellhop snapped, picking up my duffel in one hand and—turning precisely, like a drill sergeant—reaching for Mom's suitcase with the other. As he pointed to her bag, he said, "I'll bring that to your room, ma'am. Please leave it right here."

Since the readers can see and hear the bellhop being stiff and courteous in the second version, they don't need to be told how he acted. They can draw the conclusion themselves.

☙ PLAYING WITH DETAILS

In the next several pages, you'll have opportunities to practice fleshing out your writing by adding details to the bare bones of first-draft sentences and passages. Remember to look for opportunities to show rather than tell, especially when the five senses are involved. Play with different kinds of details—descriptions, dialogue, and comparisons—until you've painted a picture for your readers.

EXERCISES

Adding Details I

To sharpen the focus on the following sentences, rewrite them by adding details that either give characteristics, distinguish parts, or make comparisons. Write at least two versions of each sentence, one with a single modifier, the other with several modifiers.

EXAMPLE

Lynn ran barefoot along the beach.

↓

Lynn ran barefoot along the beach, **stepping gingerly to avoid the cigarette butts and empty beer cans.**

OR

Lynn ran barefoot along the beach, **skimming the edge of the waves, splashing her feet in the receding surf like a kid playing in a rain puddle.**

A. The boys trashed the yard.

B. Jonathan couldn't finish the marathon.

C. The salesclerk wore mismatched clothes.

D. A helicopter hovers over the brightly lit scene.

E. The TV cameras recorded Princess Diana's funeral.

How to Get Ahead

Revise the following sentences into a story that conveys the humor created when a young woman has to think on her feet in order to get out of a sticky situation. Add details of your own that will make the scene more vivid. You might think about what the man looks like, how Kym reacts, what he and Kym sound like. What do you think Kym is doing when the man walks up?

1. A man walked up to Kym.

2. Kym worked as a clerk at a supermarket.

3. The man asked Kym about the price of lettuce.

4. Kym told the man that lettuce cost 99 cents a head.

5. The man complained.

6. He said the lettuce would spoil before he could eat it all.

7. He said he wanted only half a head.

8. Kym said she couldn't sell him half a head.

9. Even after this, he asked again.

10. Then he asked to see the store manager.

11. Kym walked to the back office to tell her boss.

12. She didn't realize [this].

13. The man was following her.

14. "Sorry to bother you, Ms. Lumberger," Kym said to her boss.

15. "But some idiot guy wants to buy a half a head of lettuce."

16. Kym turned around.

17. Kym pointed to the front of the store.

18. Then Kym saw [this].

19. The man was right behind her.

20. "And this nice gentleman wants to buy the other half," Kym said.

Making Showing Statements

Rewrite the telling statements below so that they become showing statements. Make the showing statements so vivid that readers can sense the actions and ideas without being given the telling statement.

EXAMPLE

The senator spoke to the reporter defiantly.

The senator shouted, "Baloney," to the reporter, punctuating her remarks by sharply bashing her fist on the podium.

A. The radio blared.

B. The school halls were tense.

C. The kitten was playful.

D. The holiday fireworks were spectacular.

E. The artist labored over the drawing.

Zombie High

The following sentences tell readers about teenagers' sleep patterns. Combine the sentences into an explanatory draft that informs readers about teenagers' sleep habits. You will have to add details drawn from your own experiences and observations to make the draft come alive; feel free to include brief examples, anecdotes, or dialogue exchanges.

1. The student falls asleep at his desk.

2. The teacher finds an amusing way to wake him.

3. The class laughs.

4. A mom or dad stands outside a ninth grader's bedroom.

5. The frustrated parent speaks loudly once again.

6. The frustrated parent is trying to awaken an oversleeping son or daughter.

7. These are familiar pictures to American teens.

8. Why do these events happen so often?

9. Why do teens love their sleep so much?

10. Sleep researchers say that it isn't laziness.

11. Sleep researchers say that adolescents simply need more sleep.

12. Sleep researchers say teens need at least nine hours of sleep.

13. Sleep researchers define "adolescents" as those between eleven and twenty-two years of age.

14. Sleep researchers offer a scientific explanation for teens' sleep patterns.

15. In late puberty the body secretes the sleep-related hormone melatonin at a different time than it normally does.

16. This changes the circadian rhythms that guide a person's sleep/wake cycle.

17. Circadian rhythms are biological functions that vary according to the time of day in response to daylight or dark.

18. Staying up very late and sleeping very late is a common pattern for adolescents.

19. They like to stay up late for a number of reasons.

20. Many families have at least one such "sleepyhead" teen.

21. Many families have stories to tell about their "sleepyhead" teen.

22. Unfortunately, most high schools start very early in the morning.

23. They start at the very time teens need an extra hour of sleep.

24. Perhaps it's time for educators to reconsider high school hours.

25. After all, we don't want the halls populated by sleepwalking zombies, do we?

Adding Details II

To sharpen the focus of the following sentences, revise them by adding details that give characteristics, distinguish parts, or make comparisons. Write at least two versions of each sentence, one with a single modifier, the other with several modifiers.

EXAMPLE

The satellite went out of control.

The satellite went out of control, **pirouetting like a weightless dancer marking infinite time.**

OR

The satellite went out of control, **rising, dipping, and looping haphazardly until it reentered the atmosphere in a fiery flash.**

A. The yellow Labrador pranced around the park.

B. The protesters stood at the entrance to the waste dump.

C. The tricycle sits rusting in the yard.

D. The crowd watched the firefighters.

E. Ramon sat entranced in front of the computer screen.

Alternative Sports

Combine the following sentences into an informative essay about alternative sports. Use details from the list that follows the numbered sentences in order to make your draft show rather than merely tell. Choose only the details you think will be most informative; feel free to add details from your own experience if you have watched or participated in alternative sports. You might want to change the title of your draft to reflect what you have focused on.

1. Some Americans think [this].

2. Team sports are becoming a thing of the past.

3. They point to the mushrooming popularity of alternative sports.

4. Magazines devoted to alternative sports appear on the newsstand.

5. ESPN's X Games, the "Olympics" of alternative sports, began in 1995.

6. Attendance at the X Games increased rapidly.

7. Television ratings for the X Games increased rapidly.

8. Increasing numbers of Americans participate in alternative sports.

9. Sites for alternative sports are quite different from the grassy stadiums of team sports.

10. Alternative sports take place on the street.

11. Alternative sports take place in half-pipes.

12. Alternative sports take place in the water.

13. Alternative sports take place in the air.

14. Alternative sports take place on rock walls.

15. Some alternative sports are also called extreme sports.

16. They have a high risk factor.

17. The X-venture racing competition is the most extreme sport in the X games.

18 It sounds tame compared to some other really extreme sports.

19. Extreme sports include slack lining, foot-launched flight, and base jumping.

20. Athletes who participate in slack lining, foot-launched flight, and base jumping have been called gravity slaves.

21. Gravity slaves love the risk of defying gravity's pull.

22. Alternative sports may not be risky to everyone.

23. Some stockbrokers are advising their clients to invest in alternative sports equipment, fashion, and apparel manufacturers.

24. How much longer will these sports remain "alternative"?

- Two hundred thousand spectators watched the 1997 X Games.
- More males age twelve to thirty-four watch the X Games on TV than any other sporting event.
- *Gravity Magazine* covers extreme sports.
- More than 9 million Americans participate in skateboarding.
- Sky surfing involves parachutists performing stunts in free fall while one of the team videos their routines from a helmet-mounted camera.
- Aggressive in-line vert skaters perform their routines inside half-pipes.
- Bicycle stunt riding takes place inside half-pipes.
- Street lugers race down city streets on flimsy sleds.
- Barefoot ski jumpers do not use water skis.
- Wake boarders use the wake of their motorboats to leap ten to twelve feet into the air and perform acrobatic stunts.
- Sport climbers race to the top of climbing walls.
- X-venture racing requires three-person teams to cover 270 miles in six days across water, desert, and mountains by hiking, climbing, and kayaking.
- Slack lining resembles tightrope walking except that the athlete walks on nylon webbing instead of a cable.
- Foot-launched flight includes hang gliding and paragliding off mountains and cliffs.
- Base jumpers leap off tall buildings and bridges, wearing a parachute.
- One base jumper leaped off the world's highest tram above Chamonix in the French Alps, free-falling for twenty-six seconds.

INDEX

Page numbers in *italics* refer to the main discussion of a term.